BORDERLINE

Borderline: A Traditionalist Outlook for Modern Man

Lennart Svensson

Copyright © By Lennart Svensson, 2015.

All rights reserved, no section of this book may be utilized without permission, including electronic reproductions without the permission of the author and publisher.

Published in Melbourne, Australia.

BIC Classification:
HRAB (Philosophy of Religion), HP (Philosophy), HRLK2 (Mysticism), HRQC (Esoteric Religions).

978-0-9942525-7-9

NUMEN BOOKS
WWW.NUMENBOOKS.COM

BORDERLINE

A TRADITIONALIST OUTLOOK FOR MODERN MAN

LENNART SVENSSON

TABLE OF CONTENTS

Introduction   11

1. PLOTINUS   18
Aesthetics. Beauty As Reality. Art. Atterbom. Logoi. Eckart. Thinking. God. Ideas. Holism

2. ESOTERIC SYMBOLISM   26
Images. Essential Reality. Seeing. Symbol. Divine. Gestalt

3. HOLISTIC TRADITION   32
Neo-Platonism. Hermeticism. Vitalism. Connections. Linneaus. Romanticism. Moderns

4. GOETHE   41
Idealistic Approach. Mind and Matter. Goethean Science. Overview

5. REDUCTIONISM   47
Complex Systems. The Whole. Organism vs Mechanism. The Scientist. Embedded in Sein. Eriksson. Newton. Laurency. Benzene Ring. Balogh. Standing Waves. Sheldrake. The Self. Huxley

6. SCIENCE APPROACHING HOLISM — 63
Brian Green. Quantum Mechanics. Parallel Universes. Andrei Linde. String Theory. Holistic Paradigm

7. ANTHROPIC PRINCIPLE — 70
Observer. Perennialism. Reflection. God. Paul Brunton. Dreamworld. Consciousness

8. THE METAPHYSICS OF PHYSICS — 75
Characters. Eriksson Again. Synergetics. New World View

9. FISCHER'S VISION — 81
Sein. Structures. Symbols

10. THE CREATION — 85
I Am. The Beginning. Gnostic Perspective. Rigveda

11. VEDIC PHILOSOPHY — 90
Divine Light. One God. Spirit

12. STEINER'S CHRISTOLOGY — 93
Logos. The Beginning. Logos Lives On. Template. Subtle Bodies. Solar Angel. Spirit of the Sun. Christ and Identity. Etheric Body. Coup de Lance. Septenaries. From Jesus to Christ. Reborn Divine Spirit. I Am. Mankind's Spiritual Development

13. FURTHER INQUIRIES INTO STEINER'S CHRISTOLOGY — 108
Carlgren. Secret Knowledge

14. HOLISTIC ETHICS: SOME NOTES   114
To Be Good. Compassion. Truth. Will. Taking Control. Holism. Here and Now. A Core Concept. Affirmation

15. ON EQUANIMITY   124
Being Calm. Pneuma. The Gita. Western Strains

16. ON ACTING   130
Having to Act. Slave on the Triumphal Chariot. Napoleon. Get Going. Jünger. NAMO. Castaneda. Warrior Mindset. RAWALTAFA

17. THE CHAOTIC MINDSET   139
Zeitgeist. Reservations. No War. Avoiding Chaos. Sentimental Materialism

18. JUNG: INTEGRATING THE OPPOSITES   145
Individuation. Mandala. Mystic. God. Recent Reception. Literature. Fantasy. Integrating the Shadow. Campbell

19. NIETZSCHE: NO ORDINARY ATHEIST   156
Safranski. Compassion. Nihilism. Atheism. Style. Dionysus. Evola on Nietzsche. Tragic Optimism. The Nihilist Outlook. Being Free. No One Escapes Metaphysics. Life and More Than Life. Putting Nietzsche on His Feet.

20. EDITH SÖDERGRAN   173

21. T. S. ELIOT   180

22. CASPAR DAVID FRIEDRICH   187

23. INTEGRAL ARTISTRY   194
Harmony Through Conflict. Holistic Aesthetics. Structure = Freedom. See the Light. Get Going

24. SWEDENBORG   199
Materialist Beginnings. Bergquist. The Text. Dream Diary

25. ERNST JÜNGER   203
Eumeswil. Jünger Bio. War Diary. Symbolic Worldview. God

26. THE ESOTERIC WORLD-VIEW   207
Reality Is Spiritual. Order From Above. Energy. Flame of Inspiration. Ontologic Hierarchy

27. APHORISMS   214

CODA   222

WORDLIST   223

SOURCES   226

INDEX OF PERSONS   231

ABOUT THE AUTHOR   233

INTRODUCTION

This is borderline—an effort in making a synthesis of everything, creating an integral concept of Man, God and the Universe. *Borderline* is a venture in uniting Man with God, action with being, East with West and mind with matter. In this study I'll fuse ethics with ontology, the detail with the whole, body with soul and reason with intuition. In the following pages I'll try to integrate the traditional with the modern, the active with the inactive and the spirit with the symbol.

This might sound ambitious. And I fully acknowledge this.

The ontological starting point of *Borderline* is the western spiritual tradition, the Perennial Thought originating with Plato and Plotinus. It's about seeing the Original Picture in the depiction; to look the idea in the eye, seeing the soul in the mirror. Seeing the divine in the everyday, the detail in the whole and the whole in the detail. The purpose of *Borderline* is that this idealism is still a viable train of thought, essential for today's spiritual life and outlook, not just some academic pastime.

Greek idealism is not the only base of *Borderline*. The Vedic philosophy of India and esoteric Christianity, are also part of the current spiritual background. I adhere to the Primordial Tradition, the age-old tendency to see the essence of reality as residing in the invisible. Matter and tangible objects have a lower degree of reality than the soul, the spirit and the immaterial side of life such as ideas, songs and invisible but guiding patterns of all kinds. This is the Perennial World-view, detectable in western and eastern thought, in philosophies and the core values of all religions. (As for the definition of "perennial," "primordial" and other concepts used in this study, see the Word List.)

I'll elaborate on this in the following pages. And the gist of the world-view I present in the book is this: I'm a holist acknowledging the big picture, whether it concerns the *microcosm* (Man, objects, artworks) or the *macrocosm*, that is, the Universe. On every level of reality I acknowledge wholes. *Borderline* will show you this in a synthesis spanning from ancient times to contemporary times, from Greek thought and Hinduism to Christianity, from rationalism to art, and from idealistic philosophy to modern science.

Wholes are one theme for this study; I tend to focus on systems, synergies and harmonies. So why then the "Borderline" title for the book? This is associated with duality, or meeting a border and not being able to go beyond it. But I do go beyond: *Plus Ultra* is my motto. But to integrate the Borderline concept into holism you could say: on the Borderline I occupy a circle, a mandala. There I sit and meditate, trying to unify Man with God, action with being, the detail with the whole and the symbol with the spirit. So join me in the Gray Area—an area difficult to define but nontheless real, an area where the whole is implicit, a crossroads of concepts and approaches. A *No Man's Land* that in a moment can turn into an *Everyman's Land*.

This I hope for very much. But there's another way of fusing the Borderline concept with holism, with the gray area venture that this book may be. Specifically, I'm thinking of psychology where a "borderline case" is a person with a diagnosis impossible to be covered by merely one label—so instead he's classified as a *borderline personality*, being a mixture of "schizophrenic, paranoid, megalomaniac" or some-such. For a book like this, a philosophical essay, a study in *integral perennialism*, it might be a little odd to borrow a concept from psychopathology. But I have no taboos in that direction. I'm not romanticizing mental illness. Neither do I shy away from aspects of it. Truly, one of the symbol figures that guided me when writing this book was the Swedish poet Gustaf Fröding (1860-1911). At the end of his life he had a project of uniting and reconciling light with dark, evil with good and the temporal with the perennial, a philosophical venture trying to go beyond conventional morality, a holistic mission inspired by Nietzsche. Even before this Fröding had shown signs of mental instability and this endeavor didn't make him saner. And in itself this late period Fröding project didn't quite cohere, not engendering any triumphant results such as Nietzsche's *Zarathustra* book. But Fröding did write some alluring poetry in this vein. And in having the Primeval Force symbolized in the Holy Grail he visited an area where even such luminaries as Julius Evola and Rudolf Steiner have gone. Fröding didn't use the word "energy" but his elaborations pointed in that direction, the idea that God in the form of energy is everywhere.

Fröding isn't treated in this book of mine; he gets no separate chapter in the treatise proper. But Steiner does. And Evola's reading of Nietzsche is covered in the proper chapter. And to mention some other symbol figures of the holistic, integral kind that have inspired this book and that I delve into below, we have names such as Carl Jung, Goethe, C. D. Friedrich, T. S. Eliot, Swedenborg and Plotinus. Details on where I examine them and their thought follow. And in brief, all of these knew that you have in some way— if only conceptually—to integrate the dark with the light in order to outline a broad, far-reaching, all-encompassing *Weltanschauung*. They all knew of this attitude: *we need contrasts to see wholes.*

This is the motto for the integral aspect of this book: to see contrasts—black/white, yin/yang—in order to grasp the big picture. In addition to this and the basic ontological theme this book covers the role of metaphysics in modern science, it touches on ethical issues and it says something of poetry and art, all of it with some footing in holism and spirituality. This book is a borderline case of philosophy, integrating power with spirit, Man with God, the detail with the whole and the spirit with the symbol. My main errand is to describe some classical and traditional but at the same time topical concepts, and anchor them in authoritative studies and documents. But if there's an underlying tendency to this book it might be covered by the above mentioned motto, *Plus Ultra*. Plus Ultra is Latin and means: "further beyond" and in a broader sense "expanding, progressing, going Beyond the Beyond". Conceptually, this might be what humanity has to learn now, at this point of history: to virtually "go beyond," to raise ourselves from materialism and embrace spirituality. This means to acknowledge the holistic paradigm, to acknowledge mind over matter, to realize how the invisible side of reality affects the visible by way of patterns, theories, ideas. We come here to learn and not wishing to raise yourself beyond what you are, to me seems immature.

We need to go spiritually Beyond and this theme is present in *Borderline*, explicitly and implicitly. Another way of looking at the purpose of this book is that it's an attempt at building a bridge—a bridge between two cultures, the technological-scientific on the one hand and the humanistic-philosophical on the other. This existence of two clashing cultures was highlighted by the British physical chemist C. P. Snow (1905-1980) in the 50s. And *Borderline* is, in a way, an attempt at unifying these cultures. This study aims at joining the metaphysics of Plotinus with art, ethics and modern science, leading us to a holistic world-view, a *Weltanschauung* of order, beauty and harmony, not the divided, disorganized, nihilistic mess we see today. Integrity, order and harmony is the way of the future, not a continued rule of reductionism, this regimen of division, partition and narrow specialists, "knowing almost everything about almost nothing".

This is an essay. The French word *essai* means "attempt". This is no deductive lecture, no rigid system. This is an attempt at a serious discussion. I'm trying to catch an elusive phenomenon in the gray area between art and science, action and being, transcendence and immanence. If I'm wrong and out of line, then say so. But I would also like to ask the reader to step up a notch and match the level of this overview. There's order and there's chaos and if you want to gain order in your life and outlook, you have to *will* to have it. Thus: try being a man with order inside. Don't succumb to the Chaotic Mindset (chapter seventeen), especially not when reading this book. Try instead to be an Aristocrat of the Soul, as Julius Evola called it. Such an Aristocrat can have more than one thought in his head at once, he isn't offset by any "trigger word" and he thinks before he speaks.

If the reader of this book is of the Chaotic Mindset, a nihilist materialist with Chaos inside, then there's the risk of my creed being misinterpreted. But if the reader is an Aristocrat of the Soul, a man with Order inside, then the risk of this is not so great. Why, he might even grasp a notion or two.

Any person can buy and read this book. It isn't aimed at professional thinkers per se. But my imagined reader is "the educated man on the street," an everyman with some sense of spiritual elevation, some sense of order inside him. This is sorely needed in these materialistic, nihilistic times.

Borderline is a crossroads of ideas, a gray area of human conceptual striving. *Borderline* is an this attempt at *integral esotericism*.

〜

The structure of this book is the following.

The most important figure in *Borderline* is the Greek esotericist Plotinus and he's presented in chapter one. Chapter two delves into the symbolic aspect of his thought. Chapter three makes an overview of the perennial, holistic tradition that Plotinus and Plato spawned.

In chapter four another key figure for the book is presented: Johann Wolfgang von Goethe. He was both part of the Plotinus-Plato tradition and a man having ideas on natural science. This opens for the following five chapters, discussing modern science in the crossfire between reductionism and holism. Plotinus resurfaces in chapter nine where a modern study of his thought is presented, an essay showcasing his relevance for today's science.

The following four chapters take a closer look on mysticism in the east and the west, aspects of Perennialism that I find essential. Then I discuss some ethical ideas, moral issues of today within the framework of Perennial Thought.

A third key figure of this study (along with Plotinus and Goethe) might be Carl Jung, a man knowing how to integrate opposites, a Borderline thinker indeed. He's presented in chapter eighteen. Then I look into the idealistic and holistic sides of Friedrich Nietzsche, another gray-area figure. I'll try to show that he wasn't a thread-bare nihilist-materialist as some may think. The Swedish poet Edith Södergran, a disciple of Nietzsche, comes next and is followed by a look into the thought of another poet, T. S. Eliot. Then I give you a chapter on the painter Caspar David Friedrich, an eminent example of a spiritually and perennially footed artist. This artistic section is topped off with a look into *Integral Artistry*, containing a theory of art.

Next in *Borderline* we encounter the Perennial side of two memorable figures, Emanuel Swedenborg and Ernst Jünger. Then a sort of summary is delivered in chapter 26, entitled "The Esoteric World-View". The book is rounded off by some aphorisms and a Coda. And lastly, a word-list. This gives you an overview of some specific concepts I use in this study.

~

You're reading *Borderline,* an essay in the gray area between philosophy, natural science, art and morals. The intended subtitle for it is: "a traditional outlook for modern man". This book is a statement, a survey in integral esotericism for contemporary man. As concerns the time of its publishing, you could say that it's an essentially peaceful time. This might seem odd to some but I mean it like this: since 11/11 2011 the prospect of all-out war is over, it's done with; there won't be any major war because essentially, the

Zeitgeist now is against it. Reportedly, the *Kâli Yuga* of materialism and death has now given way for *Sat Yuga*, an era of truth, science and beauty, of will-driven spiritual elevation like never before. But not everyone believes this. Rather many people today go around like crazy waiting for a war or some cosmic deluge.

This is rather odd—my role, of preaching peace and having no one believing it. The book you're about to read isn't expressly about propagating peace—but it is about stressing the need for spirituality and esotericism on all levels of society—in art, science and ethics. The message on the following pages, on seeing man and nature in a holistic way, is sorely needed today. The ideas aren't new, as intimated they have a firm footing in tradition, but the way they are presented makes them easier to relate to for modern man. This, at least, is what I hope; this has been the guiding idea when writing *Borderline*.

Härnösand 20/6 2015

LENNART SVENSSON

1. PLOTINUS

THE ONTOLOGY OF Plotinus (204-270 CE) is a centerpiece of western esotericism. The following chapter is mainly to be seen as "some informal notes" on the subject. I will, however, try to catch the gist of Plotinus' world-view so that the educated reader of today gains clarity in the matter. This will serve as a kind of ontological foundation for this book, *Borderline*, with its intent of being a survey of esotericism for modern man and contemporary society. A note as for the terminology: below, I use "idea" and "form" as synonyms.

Aesthetics

Aesthetics is a central element of Plotinus' ontology. An aesthetic approach can give us a first glance of Plotinus' world-view. For instance, Plotinus teaches us to see the world as a *beautiful work of art*.

The world is an artwork, deliberately and intelligently created. Consequently, all the things in the world can be seen as minor artworks. Beauty is a measure of how real a thing is: the more beautiful, the more real and essential.

With Plotinus you could say: *the objects are beautiful inasmuch as they express the idea.* Every object, creature and being are expressions of some idea. The ideas are embodied by the things as well as man is an embodied soul. The soul is the *sine qua non* of man, the idea is the *sine qua non* of the inanimate object.

Another way of expressing the concept of "the world as an artwork" is: "Nature and art both create with the ideas as patterns." Yet another one is: "What nature writes obscurely we can see clearly in art." This Plotinus tells us in his treatise *The Enneads*.[1] You could say: Plotinus loved the world because it was a mirror of the World of Ideas. Divine beauty and goodness were present in the temporal things, as a shadow. To love the material world was therefore to love God.

Beauty As Reality

Plotinus meant: the beautiful is the real. Beauty was equal to richness of being, of *Sein*, of *esse* (Latin: present active infinitive of "sum", to be). "The beautiful in this world points to the best in the other world," Plotinus maintained.

What, then, is beauty? One aspect of it is *symmetry*. Or rather, the life that is expressed in symmetry is beautiful. God is the source of life and beauty, not bodies themselves. This is what Plotinus meant.

The world is in tune with itself. Harmony exists, the consonance of life and light is there for all to see. The material world may be temporal and have its elements of decay and death, it may be a creation "out of necessity," of *ananke*, but it's still a beautiful world. Ugliness and "material indulgence" ("sin") only exist in the mind of individuals, not in creation as a whole.

Beauty emanates from higher ontological dimensions, primevally beautiful worlds, reaching down to lower realms. The Higher is structured by the lower.

---

[1] Plotinus quotes in this chapter are translated from Rudberg's 1927 Swedish selection. For details about this and other documents, see the list of sources.

Art

I've been speaking of Plotinus' concept of art as an ontological aspect. In this respect it's a known fact that Plato (428-347 BCE), the father of idealism, didn't endorse art as a viable enterprise. He saw artistic endeavors (sculpture, painting, poetry etc.) as mere copies, in fact, as copies of copies, depictions of nature which, for its part, already was an imperfect copy of the World of Ideas.

Returning to Plotinus, he was more positive toward artistic endeavors. Again: "What nature writes obscurely we can see clearly in art," Plotinus said in *The Enneads*. God is a symbolic artist, creating tangible objects so that the idea can express itself. However, this kind of symbolic expression isn't merely done by God, it's also performed by human artists and man generally. An artist sees into the World of Ideas, then he creates an artwork giving us the idea in form, as a symbol.

To sum up Plotinus' "aesthetic ontology," you could say: the beautiful is the real. Beauty is equal to richness in reality, being, German *Sein*, Latin *esse*. Beauty emanates from higher dimensions: "The beautiful in this world points to the best in the other world."[2]

Beauty, symmetry and harmony are revealed everywhere. Creation is in consonance with itself. The Whole is a harmonious unity standing in connection with itself, sympathetic to itself. Everything is harmony, formed of opposites.

This line, "everything is harmony, formed of opposites," could pass as an informal motto for this study, *Borderline*. It intimates the integral approach also sported by such luminaries as Goethe and Jung, treated in chapters four and eighteen respectively. In a wide sense the same integration was seen in figures like Nietzsche, Södergran, C. D. Friedrich etc., all the other profiles highlighted in this book.

---

[2] Plotinus.

Atterbom

As noted above, according to Plotinus the world is beautiful. And the Swedish poet Johan Olof Wallin (1779-1839) has expressed this thought succinctly: "When so much of the beauty is revealed in every fragment of Creation, expressing life everywhere, then how much more beautiful mustn't the Source of it all be, the ever shining."[3]

A contemporary of Wallin, author P. D. A. Atterbom (1790-1855), was rather much influenced by Plotinus' aesthetic approach— as were many other artists and thinkers in Sweden and Germany by this time, like Friedrich Schelling (1775-1854). But Atterbom didn't take it too far, unlike Schelling, tending to see art as the highest state of human endeavor. Instead, according to Atterbom, art was merely to be held as *a flower-decorated maid in the courtyard*, a figure we have to pass in order to finally reach *the high priestess at the altar*.

The priestess figure was a symbol for religious philosophy, the ultimate goal of the moral-ontological quest, the realm of the Primeval Light, of God. If, on the other hand, you remained on the lower levels, charmed by the earthly beauty, there was a risk of getting stuck in aestheticism, egotism and hedonism, indulging in your own emotions and imaginations, worshiping poetry, artistic genius and your own self. This is according to Albert Nilsson (1964).

Logoi

Gong further in this overview of Plotinus' ontology, I will now take a closer look at *the ideas* (Greek singular *eidos*, plural *eidoi*). The ideas are embodied by *things*, by tangible objects. This I've hinted at above by intimating beauty and essence seeping down from the higher realms to the lower. The "higher" equals the inner, esoteric aspect, the "lower" the everyday reality.

As for the ideas you could say: the ideas give form and shape to the everyday objects. Another way of putting it is: *logoi spermatikoi* which are situated in the interior of everything, giving shape to it

---

[3] Prose translation of Psalm 449 of the Swedish Lutheran Church.

(*logoi* is plural of *logos*, Greek for word, concept). These logoi are the inner, formative powers shaping matter into a mirror of the World of Ideas. They are shaping it into an—all things considered—beautiful, harmonious creation.

These *logoi* can be held forth when discussing a prominent feature of the modern scientific word-view: *entropy*. Entropy is the idea that energy becomes more disorganized and useless by time. But along with entropy there are forces in nature creating order; entropy engenders disorder while the *logoi* engender order. The *logoi* are at the core of the self-organizing processes in nature, seemingly creating order out of nothing. But it isn't out of the blue—since these forces originate in higher ontological dimensions, from the World of Ideas. From this *Causal Sphere* order is imposed on the dead world of matter.

Entropy doesn't rule supreme, like some authors have thought (q.v. Moorcock, *The Entropy Tango*, 1981, Borgzinner, *The Heat-Death of the Universe and Other Suicides*, 1982). Entropy is part of the whole which is governed by order and beauty. Entropy actually serves the ordering tendency in nature. In the everyday world things have to die and decay in order for new structures to arise.

Eckart

The above could serve as a summary of Plotinus' aesthetic views and then some. As for an introduction to the rest of his philosophy, the following could be said. Along with Plotinus himself this section has some footing in Wald (1987).

A cornerstone of esotericist ontology is that reality is layered in ever more real strata, that Essential Reality or God radiates his essence down to these levels. Truth, Compassion and Beauty are emanating from God, descending downward; these *emanations* form the world. From a human point of view the core of Man—the Self, the I, Âtman, "the soul"—essentially remains in an elevated stage, for ever residing on a higher level. The Self always remains undescended, it doesn't really delve among worldly objects but floats in a higher sphere. This is the very Soul Spark, "das Vünklein der Seele" (Eckart), *scintilla animae*—and if you acknowledge this level of your being, this highest level of individuality, then you'll reach your True Self. In the terminology of William Blake you've reached *identity* and shunned away from *egotism and self-hood*.

Thinking

You have to search inward, listen inward: "in homine interiore habitat veritas" ("the truth resides in man's interior"). This is elementary for the esotericist attitude. And the chief inner activity of man is *thinking*.

As Wald has shown us, Plotinus maintains that the forms are intellects thinking themselves. As for the subject of "thinking," you could also say: there is no thought where there is no life, therefore, the question of the forms is a question of life. And: being and thought are identical; cf. Descartes, "cogito, ergo sum".

In the Plotinian model thinker and thought are united. The Self thinks forms, thinking its own content, unconditionally and spontaneously; this is the essence of thinking while conditioned thought is of a lower dignity. Compare this to the Kantian way of realizing a truth *à priori*, intuitively and before any empirical intermission, and realizing a truth *à posteriori*, after an empirical check-up of the matter.

In this way, Wald has clarified the Plotinian way of examining the concept of thinking. And from the view of the individual it would look like: I enter my Self and think the content of my inner mind, thereby eliminating the dualism of "thinker-thought".

God

Plotinus calls God "to Hên", the One. Of this, Plotinus, in line with the elaborations of "thinking and thought" above, maintains that the One doesn't have to think, it doesn't even *possess* thinking; it *is* thought. In heaven all is eternally present, everything is fullness (*pleroma*), no future or past exists, no shortage that has to be filled.

God is the source of *Sein*, for ever being and remaining what it is while all of reality emanates from him.

In *The Enneads* Plotinus also says of the One, that it,

> ...didn't come as expected, instead it came as something not having come. Because, it wasn't observed as something arrived but as something existing before everything else, even before reason came.

This may be proof of the enigmatic character of Plotinus' style. But the meaning is not so obscure: like God, the One is "beyond category," hard to fathom. It is primeval, eternal, original.

∼

Sometimes German terms are better than English, as in ontology. In German "Sein" is Being, ultimate reality, while the things and creatures that exist in reality are "Seiendes" (beings). In using English the German expression "Seiendes im Sein" would be translated as "beings in being," which is confusing. See the Wordlist at the end of the book for more on this. What I just said will clarify my following elaboration. Further in the divine realm, Plotinus notes about the One or God: God isn't something "being," something *Seiendes*. Why? Because the *Seiendes* merely have the form of *Sein*. And God is without form, also without intelligible form. God is neither in space nor time, neither still nor moving; he is the formless before all form. He is Esse, he is (Sanskrit) *Sat*, he is Sein.

Plotinus maintains: God is beyond knowledge, number, concept and plurality, indeed, even beyond beauty; he is the essence, the true being and substance. He is the good engendering the good and therefore "the good in a different meaning, above all other forms of good" according to Plotinus.

In Plotinus' view the soul can't say that it "has seen" God, "because, that would fit those who have stopped seeing him". God is everywhere but still one and indivisible, by the power of his will. To think about God is equal to seeing God. An individual

Self, "Âtman," can't totally be dragged down into matter (Greek *hylê*); The Self is forever anchored in God, keeping a connection with him; the Self, by its very nature, wants to go up to the Causal Sphere, to the ideas and the essentially existing. The soul spark, the fragmentary Light of the individual wants to unite with the Primeval Light of God.

And then, when meeting God, as a perceiver you become one with the perceived. You no longer think about the beautiful, you're above and beyond it, lost and at home for ever.

Ideas

The highest reality is formless and ever present. But what about the forms?

As intimated above, "form" and "idea" are synonyms in my esoteric system, as they are in some if not most interpretations of Platonic-Plotinic ontology. It's true that "form" is equal to Greek "morphê" and "idea" to "eidos". But even Plato, whose ontology Plotinus elaborated upon, was a bit vague as to the difference between idea and form if indeed there was any.

So what, essentially, is an idea? Reportedly, Plotinus meant that the idea is the "beingness" of that which is, that which remains when the qualities have been removed. The *eidos* of an object is the force by which something is what it is.

More about ideas, symbols and such in the next chapter.

Holism

The following is a sort of summary of Plotinus' holistic thought.

According to Plotinus the Cosmos is in consonance with itself. It may have been created by *ananke* and necessity but still, it is a beautiful creation. The world as a whole is law-bound, just, rational and beautiful. The good is real, the Cosmos conforms with itself. The Universe is a harmonic unity standing in close connection, in sympathy with itself.

2. ESOTERIC SYMBOLISM

A FUNDAMENTAL OF ESOTERIC ontology is the role *symbols* play in it. Concepts like *symbol, form, Urbild* and *universalia in re* are discussed here in the form of statements, giving you a clue to the esoteric world-view. The sources are the metaphysical dissertations of Plato, Aristotle and Plotinus and the akin ideas of Atterbom, Goethe, Schelling and Ernst Jünger. As for the vocabulary I find the German synonym for the *eidos*, the superior, governing idea, namely, *das Urbild* (singular; plural *die Urbilder*) congenial and have therefore used it below. For instance, the English translation of eidos in the form of "archetype" is fair but leads somewhat wrongly, to Jungian climes, and therefore I haven't used this concept so often. *Urbild* for its part means "primeval image/idea/form". Concepts that shouldn't be confused with Urbild etc. are *symbol* and *Gestalt;* they can be seen as glorified representations of the idea. Further, a *Bild* is a fully understandable example of the *Urbild*. It's true that the pair "Urbild-Bild" is rather well captured in the English pair "picture–depiction" so I will use that too.

Images

You could say: the world consists of images. These images are copies of the primeval images, of *die Urbilder*. The ephemeral has a share in the timeless by being anchored in *die Urbilder*. For instance, as Ernst Jünger has pointed out, an animal species can become extinct but its *Urbild* lives on in heraldry and astrology.

That's the esotericist ontology *in nuce*. You can elaborate on the above by saying: *das Urbild* is projected into the world in the form of a copy, a depiction of the original picture. However, *das Urbild* can still be seen with the mind's eye, in the land of dream, in art and culture, film and TV. Its substance is eternal. *Das Urbild* can also be seen in the everyday world: to the inner eye it's visible in the objects. Aristotle expressed this as *universalia in re* (the general concepts are in the things).

As I said in the Plotinus chapter: "The idea is the "beingness" of that which is". Another way of putting this, again with Jünger as paragon, would be: the true nature of the thing is generated by the Gestalt, shaping the wholeness of the object from the essence. *Das Urbild* is the super-sensuous permeating the senses, like a colored surface is permeated by the color or how water is absorbed in a bucket of sand: as an immanence, an abstract ever-presence.

Essential Reality

Essential reality is spiritual, beyond the reach of the material senses. Merely to examine (Greek *em-peiro,* from this "empirical" etc. is derived) an object doesn't say anything of its nature. For instance, sense perceptions reportedly can't be located in space. Thus, the scientific approach of "empiricism" is no fundamental of existence, it's merely a theory along with esotericism. And esotericism says that true seeing is beholding the ideas with the inner eye; we see *through* the eyes and not with them. Thus William Blake (1757-1827) in *Auguries of Innocence*:

> We are led to believe a lie
> when we see not through the eye,
> which was born in a night, to perish in a night,
> when the soul slept in beams of light.

We don't expressly see with the eye, thus, we have to see "through" it; that's what Blake tries to tell us. In the same vein the brain is merely an instrument the thought is using; we don't specifically think with the brain, the thinking goes on in higher, invisible realms, in man's spirit.

Thought isn't created by the brain, in the same way as the radio doesn't create the radio program, nor does the computer create its programs.

Seeing

True seeing is beholding the symbols, *die Urbilder* and the archetypes. Goethe said that you must carry *die Urbilder* of nature within, only then progress could be made. Indeed, everything is decided within: "I'm innern ist's getan." Goethe said this in "Wilhelm Tischbeins Idyllen".

Delving more on the relation between picture and depiction, *Bild* and *Urbild*, this can be said; a criticism of Darwin may be feasible. In nature the species are expressions of *Urbilder* having manifested themselves with the passage of time. These Urbilder or *entelekies* (an Aristotelian concept, Greek *en-tele-eicho*, "having its goal within") existed before the physical configuration, having created it, being its ideal *Gestalt*. During the course of evolution *das Urbild* has been projected into perceivable space; thus, *das Urbild* rules, not Darwinian concepts like "adaption" or "survival of the fittest". These have no formative power. They set in only when *das Urbild*, the primary, forming, species-shaping force, has been manifested.

As intimated in the Plotinus chapter (and as I will elaborate upon in the chapter on Reductionism, chapter five), reality is structured from higher to lower. Modern physics says the same: higher forms of energy generate lower forms. It can't be the other way around, this is contradicted by the laws of thermodynamics. An esotericist would say: God and order rule, not randomly working "nature," not the mere will to survive. "The struggle for existence," for its part, is merely an expression of life, a modality of evolution; it has no forming power.

Evolution is a process, not a principle. Evolution may be expressed in "the struggle for existence" and "survival of the fittest" but these are no formative forces, no guiding principles in themselves.

"Life itself," "adaption," "heredity" etc. have no shaping, creative power. You can't deduce the form of a daffodil, a horse or a pine from these concepts. Instead, "evolution" is a question of *Urbilder* over time being projected into the everyday world; this was maintained by Ernst Jünger in *Der Arbeiter* 1932.[4] *Wholeness* and *form* are the key words; the Tree of Life projects itself into observable space, the Goethean *Urpflanze* ("the Original Plant") being detectable in every plant. In the everyday world we see change, growth, death and chaos but they are counterbalanced by order, pattern, recurrence, shape and form, being projected into it from the World of Ideas, that which can also be called the Causal Sphere. (More critique on Darwinism is given in chapter five when I look into the ideas of Rupert Sheldrake.)

Goethe, for his part, had an eminent ability to see the wholeness of phenomena in the natural world. For example, he rejected the attitude of "what came first, the hen or the egg" or "the horns as a tool used by the bull"; instead, this was all the question of holistic phenomena. In short, Goethe was inspired by the symbolism and world-view of Plotinus. More on Goethe's holism later, in chapter four. Here I will only say, there is tangible proof of Goethe having read Plotinus, the figurehead of this book. We here have the Ennead line of the eye having to be sun-like in order to see the sun, and a Goethe poem based on this is: "Wär nicht das Auge Sonnenhaft, / die Sonne könnt es nie erblicken; / läg nicht in uns des Gottes eigne Kraft, / wie könnt uns Göttliches entzücken?" ("Were not the eye itself a Sun / no Sun for it could ever shine; / by nothing Godlike could the heart be won / were not the heart itself divine.")

---

[4] According to Kranz p 42.

Symbol

The objects exist so that the idea can express itself. The visible world is a symbol of the invisible world. In the last lines of the play *Faust* Goethe said: "Alles vergängliche is nur ein Gleichnis." This means: the perishable, ephemeral, temporal objects are mere approximations of the Eternal Ideas, more or less perfectly mirroring their divine origin.

The object is a simile or metaphor of the ideal Gestalt. The temporal individual or specimen is an impermanent representation of the archetype—a more or less accidental phenomenon, a chance depiction of the eternal picture, the essential idea. The temporal individual shares in the eternal reality of *das Urbild*, and when that temporal specimen is gone only the Gestalt remains, the essence of the role that the specimen has been playing. You could say: when the individual specimen is born it becomes part of the whole as an interpretation of it, as a temporal example of the eternal idea.

To again use the approach of Jünger, he once said: the object is transformed into a symbol when inner value and being shines through it. There is substance "under the surface," *essentia* beyond the *accedentia*, the everlasting beyond the ephemeral, the permanent beyond the impermanent. It's about seeing the world symbolically, as in a lucid dream, for there everything is symbol.

In English we have the expression, "I see" which equals I understand. To know is to see beyond the everyday world, beyond the ephemeral into the eternal, to the realm of the ideas. *Das Urbild* is intuitively discerned, "seen in the eye," whereby the temporal becomes symbol—and then everything becomes enlivened, like on the first day.

Essentially, matter is the expression of something ideal, the mirror of eternal ideas. Put differently: the form is there for life to express itself. Matter is enlivened by the spirit; joy emerges in the meeting of life with form. An esotericist is able to see life in the form and the spirit in matter, seeing the objects enlightened by the Flame of Eternity.

Divine

Indeed, it may be possible to discuss esoteric symbolism without mentioning "God". But personally I have no problem in associating the eternal with the divine. I'm a syncretist and I acknowledge the Eternal Light in many forms, be they Christian, Vedic, Gnostic or whatever. This book is proof of that.

As mentioned in chapter one, Plotinus called the Ultimate Reality *to Hên*, "the One". The eternal forms can be said to exist in the mind of this *to Hên* or God. "God, lead us to the silent chamber where you're pondering the objects," as Edith Södergran said. The ideas are the thoughts of God. As God is eternal, immortal and invisible, so are the ideas; as he is the ultimate embodiment of life, so are the ideas. We are co-creators with God in a world of forms.

Gestalt

In the introduction to this chapter I said that a *Gestalt* is a sort of intermediary for the tangible representations of the idea. Further, "Gestalt" is fairly established as a philosophical concept in the English speaking world. Esoteric symbolism may be called "Gestalt philosophy," if you need a label. Thus, the following can be said in *Gestalt* terms.

Gestalt philosophy is about grasping the big picture, of seeing order in chaos. It's about conceiving phenomena and ideas as wholes, as Gestalts. "The whole is greater than the sum of its parts," as Aristotle said in *Metaphysica*. For example, a triangle is more than just "three angles"; its *Gestalt quality* has a higher essence, an independent reality, a wholeness unable to reduce into its parts.

In this book I will use the terms *Gestalt Philosophy* along with *Seinsphilosophie*. I will do this in order to describe the Plotinian attitude and world-view, the esoteric approach seeing wholes and the big picture, seeing how everything has the source in Being.

3. HOLISTIC TRADITION

In the previous chapters I've discussed the ontology of such luminaries as Plato, Plotinus, Meister Eckart, Goethe and Ernst Jünger. They can be labeled as holistic thinkers. Acknowledging the existence of a higher reality, invisibly affecting the world, they employ a train of thought that sees wholes and the big picture. Hereby an overview of western thought in this respect. The main source for the following is Andersson/Mattsson.

Neo-Platonism

This chapter is about some aspects of the Primordial Tradition in the west. I look for thinkers with a holistic bent, philosophers being able to see the big picture. This usually implies a spiritual worldview. Specifically, I look at thinkers whose thought are related to Plato's and Plotinus' ontology. And this is found in Descartes (*cogito, ergo sum,* an echo of Plotinus' "being and thought are identical") and in Schopenhauer who said that in art we see the unity in the form of *das Urbild*, beyond the multiplicity of the world.

As for the Idealistic World-view, here is a repetition of sorts: according to Plotinus supreme reality is symbolized by patterns, models and "master copies" called ideas. The ideas are eternal and so are the souls of men. The ideal world is perennial; thanks to the influence of the ideas the material world has traits of beauty but is in itself darkness, confusion and non-being. There is a Supreme Reality, the spiritual basis of the Cosmos, which an individual soul can reach by a just conduct of living (*dikaiosyne*), philosophical reflection (*contemplatio*) and ecstatic vision of the divine (*ekstasis*).

This was the thought of Plotinus (204-270 CE). He's called a "neo-Platonist" and rightly so, since to a large extent his philosophy was based on the ontology of Plato (428-347 BCE). It was also based on Aristotle (384-322 BCE). Aristotle won't be mentioned any more in this chapter. But don't for a second think that Aristotle was a reductionist materialist, as some are wont to do. Aristotle too was an esotericist, acknowledging the spiritual source of reality, however, his more systematic, transparent way of thought has made him into some kind of intellectual icon (q.v. for example Ayn Rand's thought, which partly referred to Aristotle's).

Plotinus' doctrine was a centerpiece of Perennialism. He was a man of late antiquity. By this time Christianity was around but Plotinus remained within the framework of "heathendom," of ancient Greek thought and mythology; this may be a formality but has to be stated for the record. As for Christian thinkers affected by the Platonic tradition we for example have Augustinus (354-430 CE). "Bear in mind, o Lord, that my thirst after you is your own work" is a saying of Augustinus, telling us that the soul spark of a man is a reflection of the Primeval Light of God. Augustinus also meant that Jesus Christ was an emanation of the same eternal source; that's a Plotinian way of interpreting Christianity.

Another Christian thinker affected by Plotinus was Origenes (184-254 CE). In one way, however, Origenes differed from him; Plotinus namely saw liberation from the material world as possible to reach by the individual's own aspirations. Origenes doubted this, which has been called a typical example of the pessimism of early Christianity. By way of Thomas ab Aquino (1225-1274) both

Augustinus and Origenes eventually made their way into the thought of the Catholic church and, in the long run, into western thought in general. Of course, ancient Greek philosophy like the Platonic tradition also came to affect the Western world more directly during the Renaissance. Ideas of holism, pantheism and the spiritual side of nature were lauded during this time.

Hermeticism

According to Andersson/Mattsson there were two sides to the Platonic tradition. First, Plato's more formalistic ontology (the Timaios tradition, elaborating with mathematical models of the world, elements and elementary particles) was studied by men such as Roger Bacon and possibly Galileo. Along with this there was a more occult Platonic strain, as such being part of the doctrine of Hermes Trismegistus, a demigod identical to Hermes (Greek) or Thoth (Egyptian). What united Plato's ideas with Hermes' ideas of alchemy and astrology was the positive appreciation of nature, of nature as a beautiful artwork, of nature as a holistic pattern to follow. Conversely, during the middle ages a certain attitude of pessimism was around, symbolized in the depreciation of and enmity toward nature, evolving into the Faustian mood of wishing to dominate nature, channeling its forces to serve man.

According to Andersson/Mattsson this was the Hermetic ontology, somewhat akin to the Platonic: there's a hierarchy from God to matter with man in the middle. By way of *gnosis* man can liberate himself from the material prison. The microcosm of man is mirrored in the macrocosm of the universe and thus there's a correspondence between body parts and the higher, spiritual reality. A scientist affected by the idea of correspondences, for his part, was Paracelsus (1493-1541); reportedly he was also a neo-Platonic and a spiritualist Christian. His interest in alchemy made him into a pre-stage modern scientist bent on experimentation. He sought after truth both in The Book of the Word and The Book of Nature. An aspect of Paracelsus' modus operandi was his enmity toward the scholarly, Aristotelian scientific method embraced by the Catholic church, and this hostility was carried on by such men as Galileo, Descartes and Newton, the makers of the western scientific revolution. And these, too, had their holistic strains.

As for Paracelsus' holism he had a penchant for analogies. Also, he was a vitalist, having the view that the living couldn't be reduced to chemical or physical processes. He held the idea that man in cases of illness had access to "an inner doctor," a mystical, holistic idea luckily still around, even in today's school medicine. There it's called "the self-healing powers of the body".

Vitalism

Paracelsus was a vitalist, seeing life as something more than simple chemical and physical processes. The vitalist creed is about an invisible force that governs the body, not about commonly discernible physics and chemistry. Other known vitalists are, for example, William Harvey (1573-1657), discoverer of the circulation of the blood, and how blood was moved through the body by the heart. A certain mystic, Robert Fludd, is said to have appreciated this idea of a similar cycle in the macro and microcosm. Still under the Age of Enlightenment (18th century) vitalism was alive and well; a discreet life-force was needed to have "the man machine" move. Even Descartes (1596-1650) realized that the concept of mechanism didn't add up so he posited a "soul substance" (*res cogitans*) in the brain, this would be the reason for the free, volitional existence of a man.

Descartes is still held in high esteem by current mainstream philosophy and school thought. So even if esotericism and holism aren't praised and lauded in today's academia it has never been totally rooted out. As for scientific thinking, speculative ideas and school science must walk hand in hand, there's no sharp limit between holism and modern science. Traditions have lived on from antiquity over the middle ages until our days. And "the scientific breakthrough" of the 15-1600s was no simple question of black versus white, no binary issue, no question of evil versus good. For instance, Roger Bacon (1214-1292) is traditionally seen as an early advocate of experimental science and empiricism; he wasn't expressly a modern empiricist but the impulses were there, along with his being influenced by the Timaios tradition of Plato, the mathematical model of the world with particles in the form of a triangle, a square, a pentagon etc. Also, experimental alchemy contributed to the development of modern chemistry.

I will soon return to my historical exposé. But as for holistic thinking still practiced, we have the fact of *axioms* being accepted as a basis for knowledge, for example in geometry and in a thesis like, "the whole is greater than the sum of its parts". This is Gestalt philosophy and holism; contrariwise, formal logic and deduction are often dead ends, overvalued ways that never have led to any major discoveries. But spontaneous ways like *immediate insight* and intuition are still accepted within scientific theory, all the conditions for the proof doesn't have to be accounted for. In the same vein, "easily realized" (Swedish: "inses lätt") is said to be a common slogan within mathematic theorem proving.

Connections

There is no sharp line between "real science" and "speculative thought". Even today discarded ideas have contributed to the progress of science. Andersson/Mattson for instance mentions the concept of *humorism*, the idea of blood, phlegm and black and yellow bile affecting the mind, launched by Galenos in antiquity and by modern science often held as superstition. However, this idea reportedly contributed to the modern anatomy of Vesalius in the 16th century. A similar phenomenon might be that Gassendi who in the 17th century posited an atomic theory based on Epicurus; further, Gassendi is said to have seen the ideas of atomism, of particles in an infinite universe, as fully compatible with Christian ideas of the creation of the world and the immortality of the soul.

Another unexpected connection is that Isaac Newton (1642-1727) reportedly had alchemy as a foundation for his atomic theory. He was also a pious man, like Descartes believing in the existence of God; this must not be forgotten. I mean, "God" can mean many things, but for the moment I will only say that the current, seemingly prevailing western atheism is not the mainstream of human thought and never will be.

Other mainstays of western thought having a holistic wordview are Leibniz and Spinoza (17th century). They worked in the spirit of Gestalt philosophy, of unity, cohesion and awe before the wonders of nature. Contrariwise, Hume (1711-1776) and Locke (1632-1704) tended to soullessness and reductionism, essentially an aberration within the history of thought. However, Berkeley (1685-1753), still a topical philosopher, might not exactly be called "Platonic" but he was a true esotericist. The existence of the soul, God hears the tree that falls in the woods, mental images...

Linnaeus

As recently mentioned, the Era of Enlightenment had some strands of vitalism. And during this era we also had the Swede Carl Linnaeus (1707-1778). He meant that the mineral, vegetable and animal kingdoms affected each other reciprocally. This is holism, the absolute opposite of reductionism and mechanism. Generally during the Enlightenment there was an emphasis on *use*, *benefit* and *utility*, which according to Andersson/Mattsson pointed to a belief in some kind of order; blind chance and "random harvest" were not idolized. Otherwise this era was what may be called "crypto religious": nature was worshiped instead of God (Diderot, Holbach). Another crypto religious thinker in this era was Auguste Comte who worshiped Man in the form of "The New Supreme Great Being".

In order to explain how things could be created seemingly out of nothing the Enlightenment thinkers posited the *natura naturans*, the creative force in nature. Today this, in itself, is just a meaningless word. Because, an esotericist would say that the creative force in nature stems from Essential Reality, the Causal Sphere, from where *die Urbilder* are projected into conceivable space, taking shape as creatures and objects, as embodiments of ideas.

Romanticism

During the early 19th century we have an era called Romanticism. Now the existence of invisible, esoteric strains in nature and man were again emphasized (Fichte, Schelling, Hegel, Schopenhauer). These thinkers mostly affected the arts and the humanities but even physics was affected by the new holism, like the electromagnetism of Öhrstedt and the electrical induction of Faraday are said to have been affected by the *dynamism* of Schelling. The idea of the world as an organism, not a mechanism, seemingly affected these thinkers. Further, Pasteur and Kelvin were reportedly led by idealism; Pasteur (1822-1895) was also a vitalist as was the embryologist Hans Driesch (1867-1941), teacher of Hugo Fischer and Ernst Jünger. More on Fischer in chapter nine and Jünger in chapter 25 of this book.

In the deep ecology of the 20th century holism a sense of wonder lives on. The Norwegian thinker Arne Naess (1912-2009) for example feels wonder over the fact that we can feel wonder before the phenomena of nature...! Naess had his inspirational ideas. For instance, he said that we can't examine nature wholly objectively; like, we can't take a mouse and put it in a vacuum for then it's not a mouse any more, it explodes... This holistic approach makes me think of Goethe who said that a butterfly put on a needle in a collection can't be compared to a living butterfly in nature; the colors and everything are different and this difference isn't possible to describe scientifically, it has to be experienced with all the senses in a holistic fashion.

This, in turn, can remind you of Nietzsche who said: the one who hasn't smelled a rose has no right to criticize it—and the one who has smelled it loses the urge to criticize it...

Moderns

Now I'll leave Andersson/Mattsson's survey behind me. For my continued look at esotericism and holism in mainstream science, I've gathered some sayings of modern physicists from diverse sources. The following men would probably not call themselves esotericists, not seeing themselves as part of the Primordial Tradition, but in essence they are. If you acknowledge the invisible side of reality, if you stress the beauty of your equations before their congruity with the experiments, if you see the universe as an idea more than as a machine, then you're a holistic esotericist and not a nihilist reductionist.

The esotericism of modern physics will be discussed in the five following chapters, but hereby I give you this list of mostly uncommented abstracts of sayings, telling us that modern science isn't totally nihilistic. There's hope after all, you don't get thrown out of the Academy by saying things like the following. True, you could, but there's a gray area of metaphysics that is accessible both to mystics and mainstream scientists. And I'd say, contemporary physics has to move in this direction if it doesn't want to be redundant, left out in the realm of nihilism, sterility and—ultimately—absurdity.

- It's more important to have beauty in your equations than that they are congruent with the experiments. (Paul Dirac, 1902-1984)
- There are no fixed and tangible objects, only a network of processes and transformations. (Alfred North Whitehead, 1861-1947; this viable idea was then taken too far by his colleague Bertrand Russell in a nihilistic, extremely phenomenologist vein: "Nothing deserves reality"...)
- Molecules, atoms and electrons seem to perform a coordinated dance. (J. B. S. Haldane, 1892-1964)
- The presence of the universe is the background to every atomic event; there is an implicit holistic effect, a *tendency*. (Arthur Eddington, 1882-1944)
- The universe is a thought in God's mind. (idem)

As we can see these are profound ideas in sync with the holistic paradigm, a fine foundation for an esoteric school of science. A thought that seems to harmonize with this would be this aphorism of mine: "*Technology* is occupied with things that exist in the everyday world; *science*, for its part, must have the door open to "things that can't be".

Indeed: don't confuse "science" with "technology", as for example the SF pioneer Hugo Gernsback reportedly did. The Wright Bros, Edison and others, God bless them, were occupied with gadgets while a man like Einstein was moving in more abstract climes; paper and pen were his tools. That's the difference between technical physics and theoretical physics. "Physics is part of the humanities," as a philosopher friend of mine once said.

4. GOETHE

Johann Wolfgang von Goethe (1749-1832) is a key figure for the holistic paradigm. As a poet and thinker he was influenced by Plotinus. And in his scientific experiments he employed a holistic, non-reductionist approach. If I should add a critical note, Goethe completely discarded *mathematics* as a tool and a structuring element of his theories. And this remains a weakness. But still there are some interesting ideas in the Goethean science. Below I first take a look at Goethe's idealistic, Perennial thought, then I look into his natural science activities.

Idealistic Approach

Goethe was the kind of Borderline personality I cherish: unpredictable, busying himself with both art and science, with a keen eye for the divine but not afraid of "knocking on the doors of Hell to find the truth".

In the play *Faust* (1808-1831) Goethe actually told a story about a philosopher going Beyond the Beyond to find the truth, delving in the gray area of Integral Esotericism. He goes to Hell and meets Old Nick and then, free of hellish entanglements, ends up as a ruler of his own kingdom. Thus the story of *Faust*. In a related way Goethe himself integrated diverse aspects in his thought. I'll start with looking at his idealistic side. As I've already mentioned he had read Plotinus. In *The Enneads* Plotinus states that the eye has to have the nature of the sun in order to see the light, and this Goethe made into the following poem:

> *Wär' nicht das Auge sonnenhaft,*
> *die Sonne könnt' es nie erblicken;*
> *läg' nicht in uns des Gottes eigne Kraft,*
> *wie könnt' uns Göttliches entzücken?*

> If the eye wasn't solar, it would
> never be able to see the sun.
> If we didn't have God's own power within,
> we would never be entranced by the Divine.[5]

Another aphorism by Goethe is holistically clear-cut, about seeing the whole in the detail:

> *Willst du dich am Ganzen erquicken,*
> *so musst du das Ganze im Kleinsten erblicken.*

> If you want to be enlivened by the Whole,
> you must be able to see the Whole in the detail.

Goethe also acknowledged our divine nature, the idea that God is within. He didn't mean to have seen God but he maintained the idea that we can approach the Divine. We're all embraced by God, we all live, breathe and have our existence in a divinely upheld reality. This is what Goethe said to his biographer Eckermann 28/2 1831. Goethe cherished the eternal forms that showed themselves in the living nature:

> *Und keine Zeit und keine Macht zerstückelt,*
> *Geprägte Form, die lebend sich entwickelt.*

---

[5] German text after *Goethe—Gedichte*, 1949; free translation by me.

No time and no power can shatter,
distinct form, livingly developing itself.

As a side note, Goethe also was aware of this: that if you acknowledge death, the fact that the life of the physical body is limited, then you're spiritually free. It's expressed in the dictum "stirb und werde" (dying and becoming). We find this in the poem "Seelige Sehnsucht" (Blissful Yearning). Here's the last stanza, translated by A. S. Kline:

And as long as you lack this
true word: Die and Become!
You'll be but a dismal guest
in Earth's darkened room.

Later in this book I elaborate further on this intimated "memento mori" notion, of acknowledging death in an existential way. It's provided in chapter sixteen.

Mind and Matter

Now for a look at Goethe's scientific endeavors. The following is mostly based on Sällström, *Goethe och naturvetenskapen* and Bideau, *Goethe (Que sais-je)*. Generally, Bideau and Sällström take an affirmative approach to Goethe's thought although they can be critical too.

In his scientific business Goethe ventured into the same Borderline Area that I've come to occupy in this study—for instance, the Borderline between mind and matter. Specifically, this was expressed in Goethe's concept of "sinnliches-übersinnliches" (sensuous-super-sensuous) that is, phenomena that are both discernible to our senses and at the same time seeming to elude them.

As an esotericist it's elementary that some things you can observe with your five senses while some are inaccessible to them. Everyday objects can be observed and examined but some patterns and concepts are elusive. However, some phenomena are somewhere in between, like "an oil drop on a wet road". This example isn't from Goethe himself, it's from Ernst Jünger in *Jahre der Okkupation* (1948), but it illustrates the concept. For the meanderings of the scattered oil drop are somewhat amazing, they seem to be alive, they baffle the mind. I think a phenomenon like this is what Goethe meant with *sinnliches-übersinnliches*. Additional examples could be patterns of turbulence and other chaotic processes. There's order even in chaos, as James Gleick showed in *Chaos: Making a New Science* (1987). Order might manifest itself in chaos, and in the borderline between them it's a state of *sinnliches-übersinnliches*.

The Borderline character of Goethe's thought is symbolized in his aim to see the *Gestalt* both in the everyday world and ideally, both unconditioned and conditioned, both symbolically and identically. Goethe explores the gray area between Original Phenomenon (Ur-Phenomenon, see below) and type, the individual and the multitude, the experiment and the idea, the experience and *das Urbild*.

Goethean Science

With some guidance from Sällström, the spirit of Goethean science can be characterized as a form of quiet contemplation, of being part of the Creation by intuitive means. It also means experimentation: to pose questions to nature and thereby gain clarity. But experimentation and sensory perception per se don't reveal the essential truth; the discernment of the mind is the ontological judge, among the sensory data sorting out what's essential and what's not.

As individuals we're educated by the senses but we can also educate them, by way of our intelligence. Goethe called this *anschauende Urteilskraft* (the power of discerning the observed).

This is what Goethe meant. He said: "We are called to give shape to nature." We are here to ennoble matter, unifying it with the idea. The Inner and The Outer Eye, the discerning intelligence as well as the common eyes perceiving the everyday world, are both important in the Goethean approach. You could say: Goethe lives on the Borderline between the Inner Eye, pondering the ideas, and the Common Eye watching the everyday world.

Goethe didn't reduce the perceived environment into measure, number and weight. He also stressed the qualities of color, smell and taste which couldn't be reduced to the former qualities. He meant that for an essential understanding of the environment we have to study the milieu, the surroundings and relations all around rather than merely the mechanical causes. Refining our perception in this way we might reach the Ur-Phenomenon (German *Ur-Phänomen*), the simplest form a capacity appears in. Later on, the concept of Ur-Phenomenon was of some use for Oswald Spengler (1880-1936) in his study of history *Decline of the West*, 1918-1922. Like Goethe in nature, Spengler in history saw symbols and tried to capture their underlying *eidos*. He saw cultures as living creatures and not as inanimate objects. Human history is a play of *organisms*, not *mechanisms*. Spengler went beyond mere causality and saw the *soul* of the phenomena.

Overview

For an overview of Goethe's thought, these are his core concepts:

In the plant kingdom what we see are not structures reducible to its parts. In a plant the shape of the leaf doesn't cause the flower cup, the shape of the cup doesn't cause the fruit; instead, in the sequence of forms a *wholeness* is displayed. The form of a plant is governed by *das Urbild*. The archetypal biological *eidos* is *die Urpflanze*, the Original Tree or the Tree of Life, if we should talk in Biblical terms.

Further, a plant isn't like a building being abandoned by the builder when it's completed. Instead, the glorified builder remains in the living structure of the plant. God is ever present in every flower, every leaf of grass. That's the essence of esotericism, of perceiving nature as a living organism.

The following was mentioned in chapter two and now I look at it again. As for Goethe's holistic approach to the animal kingdom he meant: the problem of "what came first, the hen or the egg?" is incorrectly phrased. Egg and hen are both part of a whole, a *system* if you will, called "the living hen". The same goes for the tendency to see "the horns as a tool the bull is using". This is a wayward reductionist attitude. Bull and horns aren't reducible to parts like this. Instead, "the living bull" including the horns is a system only understandable holistically. The opposite of holism is *reductionism* and there will be more on reductionism in the next chapter.

A final indicia of Goethe's holism can be given by quoting a poem of his: "Nature has neither core / nor shell. / She's all at once."

5. REDUCTIONISM

The preceding two chapters have taken us into the realm of natural science. One of the peculiarities of modern science is to reduce complex phenomena into more simple ones. Sometimes this *reductionism* tends to oversimplification. On this ground reductionism has to be criticized since it's one of the guiding principles of today's science.

Complex Systems

I'm not the first one castigating reductionism. Others have gone before me in this task. For instance, on the net I've found the essay "The Error of Reductionism"[6] where Timothy Wilken gives us some clues to the subject in question. He begins by relating the anecdote on how a physicist, an engineer and a psychologist would handle the problem of helping a farm whose production has gone down. The engineer says that the stalls for the cattle should be reduced so that the cows can be more closely packed; then efficiency could be improved.

---

[6] http://solutions.synearth.net/the-error-of-reductionism/

The psychologist, for his part, gives other advice. Like painting the inside of the barn green to create a more friendly environment and plant more trees in the field to give the cows a more diverse environment to grace in. Wilken says that,

> Finally, the physicist is called upon. He asks for a blackboard and then draws a circle. He begins: "Assume the cow is a sphere…"

Apart from the hyperbole this gives you a clue to the reductionist mindset. Reality is reduced into models. The complicated is simplified. Complex systems of nature are disassembled into smaller parts that are easier to handle. Details deemed irrelevant are abstracted out.

Reductionism reduces wholes into parts (particles, atoms, molecules). These parts are possible to be observed under controlled and exact circumstances. Thus progress is made; this is undeniable. Reductionist science has given Western Man the command of nature, with technology he has created prosperity (if not peace). Metallurgy, chemistry and the science of engineering, electricity and medical science along with cybernetics, astronomy, biology, engineering etc. These disciplines, symbols of Western Ascension, are dependent on a science reducing wholes into parts. But the opposite of reductionism, the holistic, big picture aspect, at the same time isn't irrelevant. Why? Because the big picture implies a *process*, a system. The more complex a system becomes ("large molecules, plants, animals, and humans")[7] the less useful reductionism becomes.

The more complex a process becomes the more risky it is to exclude details. Some of these details may be crucial for understanding the process. Complex systems like "ant colonies, immune systems, brains, economies, and human cultures"[8] can't easily be reduced. They have a way of interacting with their parts, not serially as in a machine but holistically. These systems adapt and change in a way unpredictable to the reductionist attitude.

---

[7] Wilken.

[8] Ibid.

A keyword to holistic behavior is *synergy*. Wilken tells us that: "Synergy is the associated behavior of 'wholes', not predicted by examination of the "parts."

The Whole

In a general sense, reductionism has given us an affluent, high-tech society. But reductionism per se has never contributed to the progress of science. No discovery is merely made by reducing everything. The whole is always implied. The grasping of the whole comes first, then you may reduce it—and, like Descartes, coin a phrase like, "cogito, ergo sum"—and from this "deduce" God, i.e., the whole. But this is reverse engineering. Conceiving the whole comes first. This is also true for other wholes than God. Like inventing a new machine.

To invent you have to have vision, a holistic image, a concept of the whole you're aiming at. But this holistic attitude isn't normally taught in the Academy. Wilken says that "Our reductionist science teaches us that the discoverer simply assembles the 'parts' he finds in Universe into 'wholes'—whether these parts be postulates of a theory or pieces of a new invention."

To teach us how inventors really think Wilken gives us the poignant quote of Arthur Young, the inventor of the Bell helicopter. In 1976 Young said,

> There are no helicopter "parts", until after you first create the concept of the "whole" helicopter, then you make the "parts" to make the "whole". The "whole" is invented first. The "whole" comes before the "parts". The something extra in the "whole" contains the purpose and function. This cannot be determined by examining the parts alone.[9]

The whole can't function when divided. The whole isn't a chaotic multitude of parts, parts able to be measured ever-so exactly. The parts are derived from the whole, not the whole from the parts, Young concluded.

---

[9] From *The Reflexive Universe*, quoted after Wilken, ibid.

Reductionist science has made some progress in explaining the natural environment. Western man has "conquered the world" in learning of energy, chemistry, metallurgy etc. by having a reductionist attitude, focusing on the parts and excluding the whole. Now this approach has come to an end. Holistic science is now coming to the fore. "The metaphysics of modern physics" is described in a later chapter of this book, chapter eight. Here I'll continue to look at other critics of reductionism.

Organism vs Mechanism

Is the world organic or mechanic in nature?

Holistic minds see the world as an *organism*, a living thing. Reductionist minds see it as a *mechanism*, a dead object. A holistic person sees plants, animals and men as organisms, as systems affecting themselves and the environment synergetically. A reductionist sees everything as machines, working serially: first you turn the key, then the starting engine affects the spark-plugs, then the fuel in the cylinders is brought to explode, the pistons go down, the crankshaft moves and eventually the wheels turn. Conversely, an organism works holistically with the parts supporting each other in a more simultaneous, synergetic fashion.

A man having this view of organism versus mechanism was Hugo Fischer (1897-1975), a German philosopher and sociologist. Along with Ernst Jünger (1895-1998) he studied philosophy in Leipzig to the vitalist Hans Driesch (1867-1941). Fischer took his PhD in philosophy in 1921 and then worked as a teacher in Germany, Norway, India and England. In 1956 he published *Die Aktualität Plotins: über die Konvergenz von Wissenschaft und Metaphysik* (The Contemporariness of Plotinus—On the Convergence of Science and Metaphysics). As the title intimates, Fischer wants to display the need for metaphysics in the natural sciences. Metaphysics (the discipline on the nature of reality) was rather dead in the 1950s. Nihilist empiricism and logical positivism ruled, claiming to have the key to Reality. Metaphysics wasn't needed since the one and only interpretation of reality was guaranteed by the current scientism. But as we all know mere empirical observation has no value as evidence, like the impossibility of establishing a sense perception in space. So indeed, a discussion of how to interpret reality per se is needed. Like the holistic approach of Plotinus.

This Fischer shows us in his 1956 treatise. As we've seen, he stressed the need of seeing the world as an organism and not a machine. He criticized the mechanistic model of the universe, "the pool table model" of solid balls knocking each other around in a predictable manner. Instead Fischer taught us to see an interaction of forces where the *Sein* (German: being, essence) of the objects is brought into the equation. When a ball hits another it's no easy case of cause and effect. Instead, by the contact the *Sein* of both is intertwined. Because they don't exist in a dead space (as mechanist science teaches), they exist in a *rhythmitised space* of currents, radiation and invisible forces.

The Scientist

As for the role of the *scientist* Fischer had a poignant critique. The scientist doesn't have the answers to The Riddle of the Universe by merely putting on a white coat and placing himself in a laboratory. The scientist can't place himself above Reality. In using the German word for Reality, *Sein*, we learn from Fischer that the scientist like the objects he studies is merely *ein Seiende im Sein,* an Essence in Esse (Latin), another being in reality. Both the scientist and the object he studies (a molecule, a frog, a piece of quartz or whatever) have emerged from the source of reality (German *Quelle des Seins*).

Only when the scientist admits to this subjectivity, being "another brick in the wall", another existence along with the objects he observes, another *Seiendes im Sein*—then he can go on and study the world by using all the objectivity he is capable of. But in this way he can only describe the *how* of the phenomena, not the *why* and *whereby*. The latter remains theories. Reductionist, materialist theories like Darwinism and Big Bang theory are theories among others, with more or less indicia to support them. They aren't forever given natural laws. Modern natural science implicitly makes ontological claims but these claims are merely theories along with other ontological theories.

Fischer knew this. Everything is part of *Sein*, everything is governed by *Sein*. For instance, he maintained, modern science can extract and postulate categories out of reality, but for that matter reality doesn't exist of categories. *Sein* isn't expressly structured so that scientists should be able to understand it; instead, reality is governed by the spontaneity of The Source. The structure of nature is given by invisible patterns emanating from higher levels of existence—patterns like the ideas, *die Urbilder*. Only the side-effects of these can be studied, not the essentia themselves.

Embedded in Sein

We're all part of reality, part of Sein. We're all embedded in the network of Sein. We are *there*, we can't think ourselves out of it. Martin Heidegger (1889-1976) called this *Befindlichkeit*. If only modern scientists had this humility. Of course man can go anywhere with his mind; he can put himself "in the perspective of eternity" (Latin: *sub specie aeternitatis*), but there might still be some arbitrariness in such a leap. There's a leeway for interpretation that we all inhabit, both reductionists and spiritualists, and the former now have to acknowledge that. No one has a free ride to eternity, not even current school scientists with their customary attention of media and academy.

The school science world view is *one* interpretation, the holistic interpretation is another. But the holistic view takes into consideration that we exist in *Sein*, that we are enmeshed in it; in doing this holism as such becomes a more complex, all-encompassing paradigm. On this subject Frithjof Schuon (1907-1998) said the following:

> To exist is nothing insignificant. This is proved by the fact that no one can produce a single speck of dust from Nothingness. And consciousness is neither the same as nothing: we wouldn't be able to convey a single spark of it to an inanimate object. The gap between nothing and the smallest object is absolute, and this absoluteness finally belongs to God.[10]

In other words: we exist. And we cannot choose *not* to exist. Tomorrow's science must acknowledge this as a basic premise.

Eriksson

Classical physics reduced the universe into a mechanistic model. The universe was like a machine, a clockwork device. In the Swedish daily *Dagens Nyheter* in 1987 (see Sources for details) Karl-Erik Erikssson (1935-), Professor of Theoretical Physics at Gothenburg University, described how reductionism worked. As hinted above, reductionism ultimately has given us an affluent high-tech society, we now rule the world with command of energy and natural resources, and the basis of this is Western science. Eriksson took in the whole development in this respect, of technology and its societal consequences, but here I'll specifically look at his discussion of the formal, epistemological side of this complex, giving us the essence of the reductionist approach.

To begin with, Eriksson states, classical physics focused on deterministic, causally determined processes. These were principally predictable, the processes being *stationary*, *linear* and/or *periodic* in nature. This meant that in the study of nature the physicists limited themselves, but the limitations weren't a problem since during this phase science expanded extensively, there always being new areas to describe in the reductionist way. Complex phenomena encountered on the way were brushed aside as irrelevant. The general laws formulated by classical, "Newtonian"

---

[10] Quoted from the Swedish selection *Tidlös besinning i en besinningslös tid*, 1973, translated by the author.

physics were thought to apply within as well as without the adopted limitations.

However, in time the complex, discarded phenomena became more numerous. Like *turbulence*, a chaotic process impossible to describe by classical physics. Also, the structure of the universe proved to be far more complex than a clockwork, forever driving around the planets in fixed orbits. Additionally, the processes of biological life in all its variety, couldn't be understood mechanistically.

Newton

Still, the mechanistic attitude has its charm. This was shown to us by Eriksson. For instance, when Newton formulated his laws for the mechanics of the heavenly bodies, he proved that the same gravitational laws applied in space as well as on earth. This (and the previous achievements of men like Galileo and Kepler) spawned a development of physical knowledge, a search after generalities and relationships, possible to formulate mathematically. The generalization process Eriksson describes like this: limited questions were posed concerning limited problems, and from the answers generalizations were made. But this kind of generalization mustn't be taken too far. The periodic system "governs" nature but the form and *Sein* of a cow can't be deduced from this system. A cow is not a circle...!

In his article (in fact it was a series of three articles, see the list of literature for details) Eriksson also introduced modern physics and how it has abandoned the mechanistic model. But it isn't like "previously we had old physics with a mechanist model, now we have new physics with a holistic model". The physics of today (this is written in 2015) seems to be in a gray area of "reductionism-but-with-reservations". Physicists still seem to want a reductionist model of the universe—a model not acknowledging *Sein* in any form, a model ignoring the *Sein* of the Universe, the *Sein* of stars and planets, indeed, ignoring the *Sein* of themselves as human beings. Of course, Heisenberg's Uncertainty Principle told us that you can't observe without participating. In the holistic model this includes the existential dimension: a scientist can't exclude the *Sein* of himself when trying to define the *Sein* of the Universe.

Modern scientists aren't there yet. Correct me if I'm wrong, they still go on applying predictable and general laws, seemingly guiding an independently working machine. For instance, take quantum physics (created by Bohr, Heisenberg etc. at the beginning of the 20th century). On the macro level quantum mechanics is as predictable as classical physics. It's only on the micro level it's unpredictable. The measured result can't be predicted in the individual case, otherwise quantum mechanics is predictable, Eriksson says. Therefore quantum mechanics per se hasn't ushered in the holistic paradigm.

As for "the spirit of reductionism" and its possible advantages, Eriksson also mentions the *exactitude*. The knowledge of physics about the structure of matter and its interaction is very precise. For instance, "the CPT theorem" has been tried experimentally to a fraction of one to 100 trillion. Also, the law of "heavy mass = inert mass" has been meticulously tried in the same fashion, and this led Einstein to generalize Newton's gravitational theory and his own special theory of relativity (1905) into the theory of general relativity, the one he published in 1915.

This is according to Eriksson. But as for reductionism in general he means that it has run its course. Chaotic systems like turbulence and the processes of life can't be described with this attitude. The universe, the epitome of "complex systems," can't be predicted like a linear system. Even seemingly simple processes might yield unexpected results. To reduce all of reality on the grounds of a limited laboratory experiment isn't feasible anymore. Chaos theory and synergetics are needed to understand the world.[11] This points to the promising strains of modern physics which I will treat elsewhere, mainly in chapter eight.

---

[11] Eriksson in DN 87-02-03, "Trygghetens demon går upp i rök".

Laurency

Earlier in this chapter I mentioned Descartes. He seemingly reduced all of reality into the statement, "Cogito, ergo sum" (I think, therefore I am) As can be seen in this study of mine I fully endorse the "I Am"-saying (q.v. chapter ten, fourteen), but this is on holistic-esoteric grounds, not reductionist. Descartes, in stating what he did, surreptitiously made it look like he deduced the existence of God from this statement, while in essence he already did believe in God and so this all became a sort of philosophical reverse engineering.

Henry T. Laurency doesn't mention Descartes in his esoteric treatise *De vises sten* (The Philosopher's Stone, 1995). But he delivers a poignant critique of the reductionist, deductive attitude when he says that with formal logic and mechanical thought processes you only prove what you already know.

No great discoveries have been made with formal logic, Laurency says. Instead, it's the contribution of intuition, whims and *heurekas* that bring us forward. Further, Laurency means, to be *factual* is of more use than being strictly *logical*. Blindly following the laws of formal logic only gladdens Sophists and Scholastics.

Formalistic science worships *the proof* as a god. But very often, science only proves what it wants to prove. What is authoritative, what is not? That may depend on how you've formulated your questions.

In human mental activity *whim* rules, the subconscious works around the clock. Then, having reached its *heureka* (Greek, "I've found it," q.v. Archimedes), you sit down and reverse construct a system leading exactly to this conclusion, the one reached by inexplicable inspiration.

The deductions of formal logic can be deceptive. They are implicitly governed by what's put in the thesis. Formal logic might have its place as thought gymnastics, paradoxes and mind games. As for proof, however, the formal logician only proves what he already knows.

Benzene Ring

As for scientific discoveries made by intuition I have these examples.

First, we have the just mentioned Archimedes (287-212 BCE). He discovered his famed principle seemingly out of the blue. When pondering a physical problem he took a bath, and descending into the tub he realized the fundamentals of what later became this statement: "Any object, wholly or partially immersed in a fluid, is buoyed up by a force equal to the weight of the fluid displaced by the object." He got so exited by the discovery that he ran out in the streets, still unclad from bathing, shouting, "I've found it" (Greek: *heureka*, the perfect form of *heurisko*).

Then we have the German chemist F. A. von Stradonitz (1829-1896). In 1865 he's said to have dreamed about a snake biting its tail, which led to the scientist conceptualizing the six-carbon benzene ring. In time this became the basis for so-called aromatic compounds, leading, among other things, to the creation of all kinds of plastic materials. As for von Stradonitz, he was a renowned chemist before this discovery, trained to think about chemical problems day and night, so it wasn't totally out of the blue. But still, this was an achievement of a mysteriously working whim.

British chemist Francis Crick (1916-2004) is also said to have discovered the double-helix structure of the DNA molecule in a sort of heureka moment. Unproved allegations say that he was under the influence of LSD when he made the discovery.[12]

Thus, in the history of science, there are examples of how scientific inspiration works in mysterious ways. It can't be reduced to a mechanical mode of thinking, of reaching the answers in a step-by-step fashion. Instead, first you grasp the whole, then the details are worked out. Or, it's an interaction between holistic vision and an analysis of the details.

Holism is the prime mover of science and discovery, in almost every aspect superior to reductionism. Holism is the beginning and the end, the Alpha and the Omega, but in between reductionism and analysis may play a role. This I freely admit.

---

[12] http://www.miqel.com/entheogens/francis_crick_dna_lsd.html

Balogh

Next in this chapter showcasing criticism of reductionism, I will discuss the ideas presented by Béla Balogh in *Ultimate Reality – The New Paradigm of Life Eternal* (1999).

In this book Balogh goes into the nature of thought, and of thought having a more complex nature than the brain. Thus you can't reduce thoughts to processes in the physical brain. This is the beginning of an intriguing train of thought.

Balogh says: the brain is a tool for the thought. It might even be said that the thought creates the brain; not the other way around. The energy of thought creates the waves that matter, including the brain, consists of.

This Balogh maintains. The thought vibrates with a high frequency—so where does it get the energy for this? From food? Impossible; food has a too low a frequency to generate thoughts. And as for measuring brain activity with EEG Balogh discards it. EEG only measures changes in the electro magnetic field, and these can be found even around electric apparatus. So this method in itself leads nowhere.

Balogh maintains that the brain receives waves form higher ontological strata—ultimately that would mean, from the Causal Sphere. And lower, less complex forms of energy can't create higher forms of energy. Thus, the brain doesn't create thought. According to the laws of thermodynamics energy goes from higher organized forms to lower. The energy of thought creates the waves that matter, including the brain, is made up of.

Standing Waves

Balogh then goes into the subject of *standing waves*, which I won't describe in detail. But let's say: there's a phenomenon in nature called "standing waves" (like the sound from a pipe organ) and the nature of matter is reportedly another example of this, as is thought. Matter is lower standing waves, corresponding to standing waves on higher energy levels and frequencies. The stability of matter depends on there being higher energies effecting and upholding matter through resonance, like standing waves in music—and these energies exist within us. Everything is successively upheld by higher levels.

Going a bit further than Balogh you might say: everything in Reality, every creature is upheld by *Urbilder* in the Causal Sphere, by heavenly originals, by God.

The theory of *die Urbilder* explains a lot. Even in science. The concept may be speculative but I'm going to keep it in my worldview. For instance, I've read an essay by Rupert Sheldrake (1942-) criticizing the current model used by school biology in explaining life and its nature. For instance, Sheldrake is on to something when he says that DNA doesn't explain why animals and plants look the way they do. For instance, a human body cell from an arm has the same DNA as a body cell from a leg, and yet leg and arm look different. What gives the human body its shape? Using Plotinic terminology you might say that the *Gestalt* of the whole, given by *das Urbild*, shapes the organism into a well-formed figure.

Sheldrake

I've already spoken about *Urbilder* in chapter two. As for Sheldrake he doesn't employ *Urbild* or any such Plotinic terms. But he uses the term *morphogenetic field*, to explain why creatures of nature have the form they have; the term means "form-generating field". This—morphogenetic field—may be a useful term to explain the world of forms; the field exerts an invisible but tangible effect in nature. Sheldrake in this context uses the concept *morphic resonance* to explain how a fetus gains the specific form of the species when developing as it does. This model might seem vague but to conversely explain the shape of a creature by way of DNA, as is the current model of explanation, isn't a satisfactory alternative.

Current academic biology seems to be governed by the notion that biological creatures are machines. In contrast to this Sheldrake gives us a more complex model, implicating that creatures are *organisms*, more complex than machines. This is a criticism of reductionism. As is Sheldrake's notion (in *Utvecklingslära*, 1988) that materialist scientists by default can't believe in a superior nature of thought, existing above the realm of matter. Consequently, this idea has to include their own thoughts and notions. If all ideas, including materialism, are the result of physical processes in the brain, then these thoughts are mere secondary phenomena impossible to affect by the thinker.

Also, Sheldrake notes how natural science studies regularities in nature. Thus it can't explain the unique and the unpredicted or such a thing as *creativity*, which by its nature is unpredictable. The spontaneity of nature is impossible to catch in a formula. And to explain aberrations and irregularities by way of mutations, as modern science is wont to do, is an ad-hoc explanation, I'd say.

Sheldrake criticizes the materialist attitude thus: you can't understand how a radio operates, like in its broadcasting music, by looking at the mere structure of the apparatus itself, its circuits, loudspeaker etc. You have to know about radio-waves. But materialist science, in looking at an animal without acknowledging governing structures from higher ontological levels, is acting like a man examining a radio without acknowledging the existence of radio-waves.

The Self

As I just noted, Sheldrake criticized materialists in reducing everything, including the notion of materialism, their own thoughts and mental processes, into secondary effects. In the same vein you could say: the existence of The Self, the fact that man has a sense of an "I", can't be reduced. The existence of The Self is esoteric, an inner phenomenon. It's transcendental, impossible to deny by way of a lack of empirical evidence. And "absence of proof isn't proof of absence," as someone said.

Empiricism, the reductionist core philosophy, says that only what we see with our five, material senses, is true. By testing (Greek *em-peiro,* from which the term *empirical* is derived) reality in repeated experiments, using our five senses, we reportedly get a correct picture of reality. The scientist then may state that empirical knowledge is reached by the empirical method, and so the only thing that exists is the empirical reality thus gained.

But this is a circle proof. A similar circle would be: "Knowledge about the exterior world is gained by way of material, externally oriented senses, thus this exterior world exists and only this."

Materialists, empiricists and scientists reduce all the perceptions into material perceptions. They reduce reality methodologically—but from this it doesn't follow that the world is constituted in this way. They make a methodological reduction into a ontological one, thereby (as someone said) *confusing the examination method with what is examined.*

Huxley

Reductionists believe that they have the key to reality. But their hypothesis (only inanimate material objects exists, the Universe has no plan, the development of man is guided by chance) is just another hypothesis. But it is guarded like a sacred cow. As T. H. Huxley said: "It is the customary fate of new truths to begin as heresies and end as superstitions." It seems that empiricist science, once triumphing from the late middle ages and on, is now in the superstitious stage.

Studying and focusing upon the material nature was, in the era of idealism and Christian hegemony, a form of heresy. Now, in the modern era reductionist science has given us the mastery over nature, it has given us prosperity, computers and vehicles that ultimately have taken us to the moon. But another, complementary attitude is needed now—the spiritual attitude, the ontological holism, acknowledging a more complex, energetic, ordered universe.

The school science of today ought to be more esoteric. There's no essential contra-position between science and esotericism. We all seek knowledge about Reality, about The Absolute. We all seek knowledge of That Which Is, of the notions we can accept without reflection. I mean, reflection and deliberation are always needed. But at the end of the day, not acknowledging any Eternal, Higher Truths beyond the everyday world, is equal to chaos and confusion.

Order has to defeat Chaos. Light must shine forth in the Darkness. *Lux in Tenebris* would be a fine motto for the current, transitional phase, of Human Thought going from reductionism to holism.

6. SCIENCE APPROACHING HOLISM

IN THE PREVIOUS chapters we saw that metaphysical discussions sometimes appear in modern physics. Only reluctantly do the latter-day physicists delve into things ontological. But they do, they have to. And this chapter takes a look at some of these strains. It's a portrait of school physics on the verge of a changing paradigm, from reductionist and linear to multiform and holistic.

Brian Green

In this chapter I'll focus on a work by Brian Green (1963-). Green happens to be the most contemporary of the physicists discussed in *Borderline* having some opening to metaphysics. Not that he expressly embraces holism and *Seinsphilosophie*. To be sure, in his *The Fabric of the Cosmos: Space, Time and the Texture of Reality* (2007) he doesn't expressly go into the above sketched gray area of "having to acknowledge metaphysics in order to make sense of physics," but he kind of does anyway, reluctantly and by hints. So let's look at the TV series based on his book and see what we'll find from a view of holism and esotericism, seeking the fundamentals of reality in the invisible. What does Mr Green tell us about the speculative nature of modern physics, its seemingly improbable and challenging features?

The TV series' title was *The Fabric of the Cosmos* (2011). Green in some way did touch upon the surprising and stupefying traits of the Cosmos, in all of the programs. Like in Episode two, where Albert Einstein's physics was treated. Einstein (1879-1955) in his general approach was decidedly non-esoteric, more on that later, but when you look at the anomalies of time that he discovered it gets interesting. Like the discovery that movement in space slows down time. If we live in a universe created at some definable moment ("big bang"), then if two creatures are existing simultaneously and one of them moves away from us, then he ends up in our past.

The meaning of this would be: classical physics with a uniformly progressing time is an abstract ideal.

Also (though not mentioned in the program), Einstein conceptually developed Newton's notion of gravity, from a mechanically working force to a force that bends space-time. This can show us how the concepts of physics can be evolved. There seldom exists a completely self-sufficient world-view that gets replaced by a new one just like that. The new paradigm describes what the old did and then some. Therefore, the still somewhat reductionist physics of our time can be developed into holistic physics with just some conceptual changes. Like the scientist acknowledging that he, like the objects he observes, is just another Essence in Esse, another *Seiende im Sein*.

Quantum Mechanics

Part three of Brian Green's TV series treated quantum mechanics. This discipline taught physicists that different laws applies to the world of single particles (single units, Lat. sing. *quantum*, pl. *quanta*; thus the concept *quantum mechanics*) than to the world of everyday objects and beyond (planets, stars). Earlier, Newton had shown that the everyday world and "the heavenly realm," space, were governed by the same gravitational laws; q.v. chapter five.

The specificity of the quantum world is shown by the double slit-experiment. This experiment, originally conceived and performed in the 19th century, was to determine whether light was a particle or a wave. It was done with a plate with two slits through which light was sent, being registered on a projector behind the slits. If light was a particle then the projector would register a pattern of two lines, of particles going straight through the slits and effecting a corresponding pattern. If light was a wave a so-called *interference pattern* would emerge, a pattern of four lines or more. The latter was the result. Details aside, this experiment showed that particles can't solely be understood as solid objects; and if we, as Max Born (1882-1970) suggested, see them as part of waves, then some anomalies of the double slit experiment can be explained as the result of a *probability wave*. In this way the tangibility of the world is dissolved. We don't live in a world of concrete objects made up of solid particles, we live in a world of diffuse waves with higher or lower probability.

As mentioned earlier Einstein was negative to the concept of special laws for the quantum world. He wanted classical physical concepts to apply everywhere. For instance, he reportedly said, "I want the moon to still be there even when I don't look upon it." But the quantum mechanical concept of uncertainty has been proved experimentally. Werner Heisenberg in 1927 postulated that we can't both decide the momentum and position of a given particle. Heisenberg himself explained it in a simplified way that measurements of certain systems cannot be made without affecting the systems. This can remind you of Schopenhauer's idea of the world as our conception. For example, a world without spectators can't be posited, it's merely a play with words, he meant. Thus, the classical idealism of observational ontology, with the notion of the perception being performed within the observer, is confirmed by quantum mechanics. Green didn't expressly mention this but it's in the cards.

Another strange phenomenon of quantum mechanics is "spooky action at a distance". In the double slit-experiment separate particles seemed to affect each other mysteriously and the same was the case in the "spooky action" phenomenon. If you have two connected particles and take them apart, then change the spin on one of them, the other one changes its spin too, no matter how distant it is from its "partner". This has been proved experimentally by John Clauser (1942-), as Green showed us.

Quantum mechanics seems to confirm some esoteric concepts. You could say: quantum mechanics describes a world in itself chaotic, but these chaotic states are eventually "collapsed" into reality by the conception of the human will. The world is our conception, it has no independent existence. More on this in the next chapter.

Parallel Universes

Part four of Green's TV series treated parallel universes. This is a truly speculative, science fictional and seemingly improbable notion to the everyday mind. Could there be worlds existing in another dimension, accessible to us only through some portal, like the "Stargate Sequence" in the film *2001*? Do dimensions with other, more complex ontological patterns exist? Esotericists have always thought so, they call the other realms "the astral world" and such. But this and 2001 aside, postulating parallel worlds has to be done in order to explain the scientific data modern cosmology gives us.

For instance: our Cosmos is not uniform. This Mr Green stated in Episode four of his TV series. Uniqueness is not the norm. So where are the copies?

New, parallel universes may be born all the time—we live in the multiverse—if there are an infinite number of universes, there should be a replica of the Earth out there.

Theories that support the multiverse hypothesis are *inflation theory*, *string theory* and *the dark energy theory*.

First, the inflation theory. In short, the Universe seems to expand ever since the big bang. But, as Alexander Vilenkin (1949-) has found, this expansion goes on all the time, it never stops, and thus big bang is not a unique event, new big bangs seem to happen all the time, and we get a constantly inflating universe. It seems that small discharges occur all the time, new big bangs in the Cosmic Fabric—new universes are created. Next door, in not discharged energy, the universe continues to expand. Universes are created all the time—we live in a multiverse—a consequence of eternal inflation.

Andrei Linde

In Green's program the Russian physicist Andrei Linde (1948-) continued the speculation over the multiverse. He found support in the other two theories mentioned above, in 1) string theory, for universes at the microscopic level, and 2) the macroscopic dark energy theory.

According to the macroscopic approach of astrophysics the expansion of the universe should be reined in by gravity. But the expansion doesn't stop, it increases.

What counteracts gravity? Answer: an energy in space that forces the galaxies apart. It's called dark energy.

Dark energy has an astoundingly low energy. And the mystery is solved by the multiverse theory at the quantum level. The energy of the vacuum is small. If it's increased a little the universe becomes different—galaxies etc. would not have been formed.

But in a multiverse the riddle is solved. There it's reasonable with this low amount of energy, this low density of dark energy in our universe. For each separate universe has its own specific amount of dark energy.

String Theory

Now to string theory. According to this atomic particles are composed of quarks and these in turn by vibrating strings, open or closed—forming rings or being merely strings. Here the mathematics required these extra dimensions above our usual three, maybe nine or more. The strings must vibrate in more dimensions than the normal three; length, depth and height.

The extra dimensions are curled, wrapped up in themselves. They are too small to be seen. The vibrations of the strings are caused by the extra dimensions. The strings may be termed "the DNA of the universe".

Should there perhaps be posited ten raised to 500 dimensions...? Do we need that many string theories...? Leonard Susskind (1940-) says yes. And this means that string theory fits with the multiverse theory. String theory describes a multiverse. String theory and the theory of inflation both lead to the multiverse.

Eternal inflation, dark energy and string theory support the theory that we live in a multiverse. Reportedly, British science writer Paul Davies agrees on this; Davies is mentioned briefly in the next two chapters of *Borderline*.

Finally, this was said in Episode four about a speculative, science fictional idea: about finding Earth's doppelganger in the Cosmos. It can be done. Because elementary particles can only be combined in a limited number of ways. A deck of cards handed out again and again will repeat certain card hands. Duplication will occur, and in the same way it would be in the Cosmos: an apparent copy of our earth could be out there.

Holistic Paradigm

Modern physicists have to believe the unbelievable. Reluctantly modern physics are getting updated on their metaphysics. They have to abandon their in essence mechanistic models, their concept of processes that are predictable and linear—systems you can turn on and off, systems that don't encompass your personal *Sein* as a human being. Modern physicists have to get used to seemingly anomalous phenomena, like parallel worlds. In Episode four of *The Fabric of the Cosmos* a professor said this of anomalies:

> Reality is not there to make physicists happy. You are stuck with anomalies and oddities.

In a somewhat similar TV series, *Cosmos* from 1980, Carl Sagan in Episode three treated Johannes Kepler and how he finally conceived his Laws of Planetary Motion. The planetary orbits tend to be elliptic, not circular. Sagan commented on Kepler's achievement thus:

> He accepted the bare facts before his dearest illusions. And that is the heart of science.

In the same vein, you could wish that today's scientists would give up their illusions of being separate from creation as "independent observers" and acknowledge the fact of being part of the whole, as *Seiendes im Sein*. The latest achievements in physics (as par preference Episode four of *The Fabric of the Cosmos* shows us) seem to say that metaphysics again has to come to the fore in the realm of school physics. So what took them so long? Why is it so hard to accept that there are no objective or random observers, no eternal laws stating that the universe is a dead mechanism? Why is it so hard to change to the Holistic Paradigm? Why is it so hard as an individual and a scientist to confess that you don't stand above creation only because you have a white coat and work in a laboratory? Why this hubris?

We're all *Seiendes im Sein*, from the smallest particle to the greatest galaxy. Acknowledge this and human thought will take a leap forward.

7. ANTHROPIC PRINCIPLE

Is there a place for metaphysics in modern science? Indeed there is. The previous chapter intimated it. This chapter adds fuel to the fire. Below I'll give you some remarks on a central topic in looking at the world: the so-called *anthropic principle*. Ontologically, this means that the world is adapted to us. A world without an observer is impossible to imagine. This is idealist epistemology, formulated for modern man.

Observer

We can call it "the Heisenberg attitude". It could be described as, "that which isn't observed doesn't exist, it only has a potential reality." What is real is what the inner mind chooses to observe.

This was touched upon in chapter five and six. In this book I've also mentioned Schopenhauer, who maintained the same attitude. To speak about a world without an observer is nonsense, he said.

This idealist ontology, this idealist way of perceiving the world, is still discussed by science. It's called "the anthropic principle".

Briefly, let's look at the Schopenhauer view in this matter. He said that "the world is our conception". A world without a perceiver would in that case be an impossibility. But we can—he said—gain knowledge about Essential Reality by looking into ourselves, by introspection. There we would find *die Urbilder*, the original patterns of everything. This is one of many examples of the anthropic principle. The world is there for the sake of man. And a perceiver is needed in order to *realize* the Universe—to, literally, make it real.

In Jungian terms this would mean: the world is a projection. Take back your projections and you'll reach a higher ontological level.

Perennialism

Supporting the anthropic principle is to be part of Perennialism. Medieval theology, Plotinus, Leibniz and Fichte were advocates of this school of thought. J. G. Fichte (1762-1814), for his part, maintained that the essence of Being is "the pure self" which is "the thought, thinking itself". And this Self projects a non-self which is the environment. For if this projection wasn't done the Self would only be a self-consciousness, devoid of content.

For The Pure Self an environment is needed as a field of action. Otherwise we wouldn't be able to act; thus, we create the world with our thought. This process is done subconsciously—so what happens if you become aware of it? Will the world disappear?

Reflection

Anthropic principle: the creation is upheld by some mysterious force, a law seems to be ruling everything. An additional thinker maintaining this was Baruch Spinoza (1632-1677). He said that there was only one possible world, this world, an idea which can be related to G. W. Leibniz (1646-1716) who maintained that this is "the best of all possible worlds". And Jackie Jakubowski highlights the two just mentioned thinkers as representatives of the anthropic principle: the idea that the qualities of the Universe is a reflection of our existence.

Jakubowski had an article about the anthropic principle in the Swedish daily Dagens Nyheter in 2004, entitled "Om pi varit 3,141591..." Specifically, Jakubowski took a closer look on two books by John D. Barrow: *The Constants of Nature. From Alpha to Omega* (2002) and *Theories of Everything. The Quest for Ultimate Explanation* (1990).[13]

So then: a perceiver is needed in order to realize the universe. The world is our projection.

The natural laws can only be as they are, stand as they stand— for with other constants nothing would exist, for example, with another value of pi. No mass and no extension: *nada*. Thus, according to the venerable Paul Davies that Jakubowski refers to, order and beauty rule the universe, not blind chance. And this order can't be explained by empirical science. And as Dirac said, it's better to have beauty in your equations than that they agree with the experiments. In the science community, the rule of empiricism seems to be giving way to rationalism.

God

Going further in Jakubowski's overview, it could be said that God has a place in physics, old and new. Today's physics may for instance see that there is chaos on the quantum level but higher up there's regularity, consistency and harmony. And the one upholding this harmony is God. Earlier physicists like Brahe, Kepler and Newton had an inkling of this as before them Thomas ab Aquino, Aristotle and Plotinus. And as intimated this can't be reached by empiricism, only theoretically. Like Einstein, who wanted to find the answer to the riddle of the Universe with a formula. Even though he didn't reach all the way. Quantum mechanics, for instance, he discarded with the saying, "God doesn't play dice." But he had the ambition to understand Being rationally.

---

[13] See Sources for additional info.

LENNART SVENSSON

Paul Brunton

Scientists dream about "a theory of everything". But we'll never find the answer strictly theoretically. We must realize that we ourselves are co-creators of the Cosmos. The future is open because will is free. And once we realize that, then we might be "given access to the quiet chamber where God ponders the objects" (Södergran).

Elaborating further on the themes above you might say: the ultimate truth is within. This is the idealist creed. Swedish philosopher C. J. Boström (1797-1866) used to examine his students by pointing at a stove and say, "Is the stove within or without the student?" The answer would of course be "within". This is esotericism *in nuce*. Among modern thinkers maintaining the same idea we for instance have Paul Brunton (1898-1981). As for perception he meant that the observation of a spruce occurs within the observer. The perception *is* the spruce tree. Everything that I interpret as the shape and form of the spruce are my own mental processes.

The materialist notion, that the spruce is seen as growing outside you, is just another interpretation—for in essence, the thought and the consciousness where the perception takes place can't be located in a certain place. This rhymes with the idea, maintained earlier in *Borderline*, that sense perceptions have no place in space.

Perception can't be located in a place, all of space exists within perception, it would seem. This according to Anna Bornstein (1988), elaborating on Brunton's ontology. But the fact that other people see the same spruce, what does that mean? Only that their minds work in the same fashion. Habit rules. We have been taught a certain description of the world since we were very young, as Castaneda would say.

Reality doesn't consist in the outer qualities of the spruce. Also, there's no material substratum for it. Because, as Plotinus has taught us, matter has no essential reality. The form, on the other hand, the pure form, the *eidos*, *das Urbild*, this is what possesses reality. Brunton: the spruce and all the objects we see is a cosmic thought we receive from a universal mind in our innermost, an unlimited, continuous Primeval Source in opposition to our discursive, everyday consciousness, a Something beyond time and space engendering time and space. It is the originator of everything but can't itself be described.

Dreamworld

Is our everyday reality just a dream? Poe said: "All that we see or seem/is but a dream within a dream"... As the dreamer creates a dream scenario, the individual creates the sensual world by the material it's given by The Cosmic Thought, by *God* for simplicity.

Therefore it would be reasonable to get to know God within, feeling divine presence in the inner mind, thus reach enlightenment and start Seeing. Thereby conflicts between outer and inner world would disappear, like those between matter and spirit and body and soul. You would experience what Jung called *Unus Mundus*, one world, a unity between outer and inner world. Thus, the world would become the dream we create, there would be unity between dreamer and dreamed. This is truly an integral project in the spirit of what I intimated in the Introduction to this study: to unite God with Man, mind with matter and transcendence with immanence.

Consciousness

In order to connect to the beginning of this chapter, discussing the anthropic principle, you might ask: why does anything at all even exist? Then the answer might be, intimated by Gustafsson (1992): if nothing existed, then no one would be able to pose the question... And in Gustafsson's study we also get to know that pi has to have its value, and the so called gravitational constant its given value, and strong and weak nuclear interaction to be as they are, in order for the universe to exist.

What, then, is the ultimate goal of the universe? To be conscious of itself, according to Gustafsson.

8. THE METAPHYSICS OF PHYSICS

IN THIS CHAPTER we'll both see some familiar names and some new ones. The theme is, as you can see, "The Metaphysics of Modern Physics". I here continue the theme from the previous chapters, of the paradigm shift from reductionism and linearity to holism and a systems approach in modern physics and science. Below, the emphasis will be on some new strains being present in looking at our world, in the new attitudes needed by natural science in order to describe the results of the experiments in a more optimal fashion.

Characters

The German philosopher Hugo Fischer (1897-1975) has already been mentioned in *Borderline*. That was in chapter five. And in the next chapter we'll look deeper into what he says about old physics versus new, and how the new physics tends to apply a holistic model instead of a mechanistic one. Here, in briefly looking at Fischer, it could be said that he's a fine example of a modern scholar steeped both in the established holism of Plotinus and the budding holism of scientists like Alfred North Whitehead (1861-1947). Fischer also had a keen eye for *structures* in reality (an ecosystem is a structure, an organism is a structure, an atom with its radiation is a structure). He saw nature as a holistic phenomenon where everything is in connection with everything else. Fischer called the Cosmos "a structure of structures". Everything is alive, every part of nature has structure and order in it, and thus every part mirrors the totality of reality.

In line with Plotinus' aestheticism Fischer touched upon the attitude of seeing the Universe as an artwork and of the conscious humans as co-creators of the world with God. We're all embedded in *Sein*, all part of the adventure of existence. In a discreet fashion Fischer's *Die Aktualität Plotins* is a clarion call for holism and synergetics, a forerunner of works by David Bohm and Paul Davies. Davies (1946-) for his part is a British physicist and writer, for instance saying that order and beauty, not chance, are what governs nature. The explanation to this can't be reached empirically. Another holistic idea that Davies maintains is that self-organizing processes counteract the effects of entropy, an idea I touched upon in chapter one. Davies has written books like *God and the New Physics* and *The Mind of God*. These aren't theological dissertations. But Davies does have a keen eye for the invisible side of reality.

American scientist David Bohm (1917-1992) also acknowledged the invisible aspect of Being. This we find in his concept "implicit order," which is another way of saying that invisible patterns rule the objects in the observable space. He pictured reality as a wholeness-flow where everything is connected and nothing is isolated. His coda seems to be that modern science has to go from reductionism to a systemic vision. This all, to me, is Plotinism expressed in modern terms, without including the divine element. In this Bohm is even more typical of the modern scientist than Paul Davies, who at least mentions God. I personally have no problem with God being an integral, yea, *defining* presence of Reality but to you holistic thinkers who prefer to do without the concept of God, I say, read David Bohm's *Wholeness and the Implicate Order* (2002).

Eriksson Again

In chapter five I looked at what Swedish physicist Karl-Erik Eriksson said about the reductionist attitude, the way in which classical physics described the world. He wrote a whole article series on this and related subjects and here I'll look at part two, called "Trygghetens demon går upp i rök",[14] a text about the emerging scientific world-view. Here we get to know that classical, old physics focused on linear, predictable, basic processes. Also, complex processes and systems could be described by old physics (like crystals) but from the 1960s and on *partly ordered systems* became a new field for science to map. Phenomena such as transition from periodic movement to non-periodic movement were studied here, that is, *chaos,* and the order that may exist in it. Turbulence was one such phenomenon. Another new field was the connection between levels in a system; this connection couldn't be studied in a reductionist fashion, Eriksson says.[15] Except for the fact that every level presupposes all the underlying, new, unpredictable elements can appear on each level.

This still might not be a wholly holistic, spiritual way of looking at nature. Chaos physics can still be performed in the common, objective fashion. But reductionism, for its part, seems to be losing ground.

Synergetics

The science of complex systems, encompassing both deterministic and non-determinsitc processes, has been given the name *synergetics*. Hermann Haken (1927-) coined the term. I touched upon it in chapter five. Eriksson sees synergetics as a venture in interdisciplinary knowledge, a way of bridging the "two cultures" of C. P. Snow, the technological-scientific on the one hand and

---

[14] DN 87-02-03.

[15] Ibid.

the humanistic-philosophical on the other. And as intimated in the Introduction, this is also what I'm trying to bridge in the book you're now reading, of joining metaphysics and art on the one hand with science and technology on the other.

Eriksson adds a fundamental aspect of the limits of reductionism, of how it tends to be mathematically impossible the more complex a system gets. In science the ideal is to describe complex phenomena in a succinct formula. The complexity of a system—Eriksson says—can be defined as the shortest possible description of the system in question. But it's generally hard to reach that singular best description, which is an effect of the Incompleteness Theorems of Kurt Gödel (1906-1978). Sometimes you can't formulate a simplifying description. Some systems are so complex that the simplest possible description of it is the system itself.

Modern science, of all kinds (social sciences, linguistics, physics), tends to study complex phenomena, impossible to reduce into linearity and predictability. You can't describe everything in a formula. In his third article in the series[16] Eriksson stresses that modern science has to be open to unpredictability and complexity. Complete rationality is irrational, stemming from an immature wish for stability, expressed in a belief in planning and social engineering, leading to devastation, pollution and the pillaging of lands and people. Chance and unpredictable occurrences can't be eradicated from any system. Eriksson says that sense and sensibility has to walk hand in hand. A unifying of heart and head, of both the hemispheres of the brain is needed. This is holism. Since the day Eriksson wrote this hasn't wholly come about, not in the academia where he was/is active, but the tide is still turning and holistic science can't be held back.

---

[16] "Fräls oss från Tomgångsmessias", DN 87-02-04.

New World-view

The late 1980s was a fine time for discussing the emergence of the holistic paradigm. One indication of this was an article series in the Swedish daily *Svenska Dagbladet* 88-07-10 - 88-07-13. In four parts Erik Sidenbladh reported from an international conference in Hanover, called "Mind & Nature". It was an academic event showcasing thinkers like Immanuel Kant (1724-1804) and sporting guests like chemist Ilya Prigogine (1917-2003), spawning discussions touching upon spirituality in the form of the Gaia hypothesis (Earth is a living organism), the Whole and—indeed—God. In other words, this was an event taking place in the Borderline between Science and Faith, rationality and spirituality, God and Man.

What, then, did this event say in the realms of holism and esotericism, the focus of my book?

There was some criticism of old physics, like the tendency of dominating nature, treating it like an object, of man imagining himself as being able to control its processes objectively. Contrary to this was stressed the attitude of participation and of regarding nature as essentially holy—that we're part of it, as *Seiendes im Sein*. This particular clause, "Seiendes im Sein" wasn't expressly mentioned in Sidenbladh's text, however, the concept of Being (Latin *esse*, German *Sein*) was mentioned by the chairman Ernst Albrect in the opening address. *Die Seinsphilosophie* has never died out in Germany, not even in academic circles.

This was covered in the first part of the series. In part two ("Hjärnan är ett cocktail party") neurologist Francisco Varela (1946-2001) spoke of perception as a process being co-creative with the Creation, and about Multi-verse, about a plurality of aspects being possible. Thus it's not only physicists that talk about parallel worlds, as we saw in chapter six, but psychic researchers too. In part three of Sidenbladh's series ("Från rädsla till en lek med många möjligheter") science historian Morris Berman (1944-) spoke about the progress of the interpretations we make of the world, of different schools of science replacing each other. Aptly he rendered Huxley's idea of how science begins as heresy and ends as superstition. (In the context it was wrongly attributed to Aldous Huxley; it was in fact said by his grandfather T. H. Huxley, and in full the line in question reads: "It is the customary fate of new truths to begin as heresies and end as superstitions.") The old paradigm begins as a fresh outlook giving clarity, explaining a lot of phenomena deemed as anomalies, and ends up closed and petrified, cracking down on any model that doesn't fit the picture.

This is where human thought is now. The old paradigm of reductionism and linearity must go and the new paradigm, the holistic, the one which explains all the old answers plus the new ones, must take its place. A paradigm where spontaneity and rationality goes hand in hand, as Ilya Prigogine intimated in the fourth and final part of Sidenbladh's series.

9. FISCHER'S VISION

IN HIS 1956 STUDY *Die Aktualität Plotins* Hugo Fischer has indeed taken the classical, perennial *Seinsphilosophie* into the modern era. More than any modern thinker Fischer has established Being, that is, *Sein* (Latin *esse*, Sanskrit *Sat*) at the center of any holistic, perennially footed world-view. If you're going to criticize reductionism, nihilism and materialism then you have to acknowledge *Sein*, the superior, all-encompassing Reality that we all live in, move by and have our being from. We can't think ourselves out of Sein, not put ourselves above it. We're all "essences in esse," *Seiendes im Sein*. Within this framework reductionism, along with its fellows empiricism and logical positivism, become absurd. The scientist is himself embedded in *Sein* and can't postulate himself above it, as an impartial ontological judge. Ontologically we're all part of *Sein*, all part of Being.

Sein

I've already discussed Fischer's *Die Aktualität Plotins* previously in this book, in the chapters on Reductionism (5) and The Metaphysics of Physics (8). Here are some additional notes on his Philosophy of Being, his way of putting *Sein* at the core of modern philosophy.

Sein is the superior reality of everything. When looking for a "level" to anchor cause in we must go to *Sein*, not to *die Seiendes*. The ultimate cause must be footed in the World of Ideas, not in its everyday mirror image. As intimated earlier in *Borderline* a synonym to the World of Ideas is *the Causal Sphere*.

This is the gist of Fischer's *Seinsphilosophie*. He also says: nature is the existing, *Seiende* structure of physical and biological organisms. Here everything is in everything; the world is a totality of structured beings, a structure of structures. It's a system of existence fields where every field holds the totality of all creation in balance. And everything is ruled by a controlling center that is ever present.

Further: where all *Seiendes* are in balance everything is integrated with *Sein*, there the human being can thrive, go forth and emanate *Sein* in the form of additional structures, that is, artworks, thoughts etc. These structures are the expressions of the individual's life and his life thus becomes his statement. This touches on modern Existentialism whose main tendency can be formulated as: being and thought must be integrated. You can't merely construe a philosophy of life theoretically, you also have to try it and test it, seeing if it coheres by performing a constant trial and error process called "living". Hopefully we get wiser and more whole in the process, following our inner lantern and reintegrating being around us as we go. Thus we become co-creators with God, heading for Our Primeval Native Place where everything is clarity: clarity within and clarity in the things, a landscape imbued in a sublime light mirroring the Inner Light.

Structures

As for biology Fischer has this to say concerning Being. A living, growing flower, for instance, expresses its *Sein* in this growing—and thereby the connection of this *Sein* with that of every creature around it. The individual flower points beyond itself, having its structure mirrored in other life forms. As for structural similarities, this is for example rather pregnantly seen in the way the cauliflower (both the whole plant and parts of it) looks like a small tree, a miniature oak.

There are structures everywhere: in crystals and plants, in the human brain and in the periodic system. "A noetic field structure" is revealed in each of these phenomena; there's a living element in nature, as we also see in Bell's theorem and the experiment revealing "spooky action at a distance" (for the latter, see chapter six). Is matter alive, do particles communicate? These experiments seem to suggest it and an esoterically minded holist has no problem in acknowledging this.

Symbols

Fischer has the ability to visualize his thought in symbols. Like when he says that old physics thought of the Universe like a *machine* but Seinsphilosophie sees it as an *organism*. Also, in focusing on the role of the scientist Fischer's train of thought is tangible, like when discussing that the scientist is merely "eine Seiende im Sein" along with the objects he examines. In these instances, discussed earlier in *Borderline*, Fischer applies something like Goethe's *gegenständliches denken* (thinking in objects). This is a tangible sort of thinking, essentially abstract but embodied in symbols.

A prime example of Fischer's symbolic thought is when he likens the world to a cathedral. In a cathedral, say, a 17th century temple with circular layout capped with a dome, the tambour on which the dome rests has windows and thus the light can seep down and *enchant the stone structure, lifting it upwards.*

Fischer says: a temple is an existing realization of its theme. The structure animates the form, giving it essence and inner value. The part is mirrored in the whole and vice versa, like in the cathedral system of vaults of varying size. The building elements thus can be seen as a fugue accompanying itself, a structure with an inner rhythm culminating in a jubilant *sursum corda*, the "raise your hearts" of the Catholic liturgy.

New Paradigm

Fischer advises us to find the cause in *Sein*, not in *die Seiendes*. With The Primeval Light as our lantern we can reintegrate all the diverse phenomena of creation. We thus become co-creators with God, seeing Being and thought as identical, Being as equal to light and life. With this attitude we're approaching Being as participants, not as overlords. This humility is needed by all, scientists, private individuals, all.

And indeed, my guess is that we'll all have this attitude in the coming epoch of the *Sat Yuga*, the Era of Truth. We're leaving behind us the Kâli Yuga of strife, division and reductionism. In Sat Yuga the holistic attitude will be the new paradigm. More on the succession of Yugas (Ages) in chapter nineteen.

10. THE CREATION

As we've seen, Plotinus called God *to Hên*—the One. God is one. When everything has been explained there remains this *One*, this God, and this can't be explained. Or can it? There are indeed some creation myths around, some narratives trying to explain How It All Began—how even God came into being. In this subject I present the following, based on esoteric theory (Agerskov, Schuré, Steiner), Gnostic documents, Vedic philosophy and then some, discreetly infusing it with my own interpretations.

I Am

You already know my basic attitude to spiritual matters. God exists as a Superior Being of Light. Man, having a soul, is part of that Light. The essence of the individual is a soul spark, "das Vünklein der Seele" that Meister Eckart spoke about.

But how did it all begin? "God created Man"—but who created God...?

I'd say: in the beginning there were four primeval forces around: Light and Dark, Will and Thought. Things got going when

Will, true to its nature, stirred and began to move, eventually unifying with Thought. This new entity also chose Light instead of Dark. And when Will-Thought had united with Light, *God* came into existence, saying "I Am" as a confirming statement.

As for creation myths this is no Superior, Everlasting Version carved in stone. It is, however, the version I choose to employ for my creed, my Borderline ontology. The "four elements, Will-Thought choosing light" part is from Agerskov and the "I Am" part is inspired by Steiner. Steiner only says "In the beginning was Logos, whose name is I Am" and this is part of the truth I see but not all of it. God can be seen as a *dyad* of Will and Thought, which clarifies things; in the form of Will God can be a *Gestalt*, a humanoid shape, and in the form of his Thought he is ever-present; thus according to Agerskov and this also is clarifying. I mean, many scholars have wondered if God is either an ever-present immanence or a perceivable being—and the answer seems to be that he is both, depending on if Will or Thought is prominent in the practice.

God came into existence. Then he took of his Light and created lesser gods (angels, devas, archons). Later, from the same light, he even created human beings. Like the angels the men were created in pairs, in duals. From Greek, Hindu and Norse myth we all know that a male god has a female companion. This isn't made up by some clever scholar "having to fill out the mythological pantheon," it's about spiritual fundamentals. For as humans we were also spiritually created as two, as male and female, in the form of *animus* and *anima*. This is according to esoteric theory.

After a start like this you could go on and say that the World developed in this or that fashion—like being an inferior, material realm where man got trapped by his physicality. And that man eventually was led toward the light. You can also bring in Legendary Lands and Lost Continents, eventually ending up in more familiar climes like Egypt and Sumer and then go on to our times. I could tell my version of that story but I won't do that, not now. Instead, in keeping with the formal, ontological nature of this book I'll discuss some other aspects of creation that I've encountered. Like in Gnostic documents. It might be confusing to you if I chose to discuss other versions of The Beginning but in that case, think of The Upanishads where many of the different Upanishads seem to give their version of how it all began. Of course, some sort of consensus exists even there. I'm not aspiring to show off different narratives just for some absent-minded, antiquarian purposes. I want to portray Perennialism. But some conceptual plurality could be allowed for the sake of discussion.

The Beginning

A fine summary of contemporary mysticism is the following creation myth. I actually don't know the source. I must have forgotten noting it when putting this down on paper once. Anyway, this is it. Note the occurrence of "plus and minus, male and female," which could be detected even in the myth where Will can be seen as male and Thought as female. Overall, this narrative is in sync with my above conception of the Beginning:

Before everything began space existed in timelessness. Then forces of negative and positive emanated, quanta of plus and minus. When they moved about each other "the Tao symbol" of entwined forces came into existence, depicting male and female, negative and positive, light and dark, hot and cold. When this movement began *time* originated, because *time is measured movement*—and conversely, where there is no movement or change there can be no time.

Forms appeared after *matter* had been condensed in the shape of bubbles. Then *spirit* was born out of space and in the meeting between spirit and matter *consciousness* appeared. Matter took shape in the spheres, having in turn arisen out of emptiness. These were the days of *evolution*, of breathing out and multiplying. Eventually the era of *involution* will come, being a sort of breathing in and return to God. This concept can be mirrored in the Jungian concept of "taking back your projections".

In short, there are some mysteries in this Creation Myth but as intimated it isn't totally enigmatic. Male and female, plus and minus, will and thought have some primeval existence, then "spirit" arises and becomes conscious thanks to encountering matter.

Gnostic Perspective

Then we have the Gnostic documents. Some of them have creation myths. In one of them we read that in the beginning, before time, The Abyss (through its thought) projected the beginning of all. He buried this projection like a seed in the womb of Silence, she who was there with him, and she in this way gave birth to God.

God is a dual entity, a dyad of male and female. Valentinus, for his part, speaks about The Unspeakable or The Abyss (Greek *Abyssos*) which is the Father, the male entity. Then we have Grace (Greek: *Charis*), The Silence, The Womb and The All-Mother. Silence receives the seed from the Unspeakable Source, then she gives birth to everything, letting *Esse* emanate, creating harmonic couples of male and female deities.

This is again like the first myth I related: primeval forms of male and female meet. Gnostic legends have a slightly different division of gender than Agerskov, but in all it seems that primeval forces existed in the beginning, as male and female, and when these united God appeared, becoming a dual entity, a *dyad* of Will and Thought.

In discussing creation you might wonder if God creates the world in order to be known to himself, realize himself; creation as an act of a self-revelation by a concealed God. This is an accepted theory in esotericism. In creating the world God somewhat partitioned himself, but this came with a purpose. The Indian thinker Shrî Aurobindo (1872-1950) has expressed it thus: "Existence that multiplied itself for sheer delight of being, plunged into trillions of forms so that it might find itself innumerably." God divided himself into individual creatures, ultimately into plants, animals and human beings too. And we, as these individuals, can acknowledge our divine origin—and in doing so we "become" God. We become God experiencing himself through ourselves. Simone Weil (1909-1943) expressed it thus: "God loves himself *through* us."

Rigveda

The theme of the Creation as an integration of opposites is repeated in an ancient Indian creation myth. In Rigveda 10:129 we read how the world came into being by *Sat* (the existent) evolving from *Asat* (the non-existent). Thus water came into being and from this was evolved intelligence. This is not crystal clear; however, something was happening in the void and then, in verse five, "...there were impregnators, there were powers; there was energy below, there was impulse above." In Sanskrit this reads: *retodhâ âsan, mahimâna âsan / svadhâ avastât, prayatih parastât.*

I follow the text here as given in *A Vedic Reader for Students* (1917), edited by Arthur Anthony MacDonell. In a comment he says: "*retodhâ* and *mahimâna* are contrasted as male and female cosmogonic principles, which correspond respectively to *prayati* and *svadhâ*."[17] Then the poem goes on to say that the gods were created after all this, the Cosmos existed before them—so who, then, can answer the question whence this creation arose? You could of course ask the Supreme Surveyor (verse seven) but maybe even he doesn't know. This reveals a certain atheistic or proto-Buddhistic trait in this poem. And I'm not into that particular thought system now. However, Rigveda 10:129 overall is an intriguing contribution to the discussion on how creation happened and it agrees with many others (see above) in stating that in the beginning opposite forces (male and female, impregnators and powers, energy and impulse) were active in uniting with each other and creating The Cosmos.

---

[17] *A Vedic Reader for Students* (1917), ed. Arthur Anthony MacDonell, p. 210.

11. VEDIC PHILOSOPHY

In the previous chapter I touched upon Vedic Philosophy, and in Perennial Thought this Vedic strain can't be ignored. The ancient Indians maintained advanced ideas in the realm of God and Man. This summary shows us that the Plotinic visions of inner reality in man were shared by ancient Indian thought.

Divine Light

The Vedic scriptures that I've studied are the *Rigveda, Upanishads* and *Bhagavad-Gîtâ*. The Rigveda was covered in the preceding chapter. Now I'll take a brief look at the Upanishads[18] and its successor, the Bhagagavad-Gîtâ;[19] the translations given are mine. What do they tell us about God and Man?

As I told you earlier in this book every man has a Divine Light within. And The Upanishads says the same: God is within. In every individual there's the Divine Light. God is the "incorporeal in

---

[18] Sanskrit text after *Upadeshasâhasrî*.

[19] BhG, Sanskrit text after the BBT edition 1983.

the bodies" (*ashariram sharîreshu*).²⁰ He is "the undivided in the divided" (*avibhaktam vibhakteshu*).²¹

God is within. "The One God is hidden within every creature" (*Eko devah, sarvabhûteshu gûdhah*).²² "God is the same within every creature" (*Samam sarveshu bhûteshu*).²³

"God is within"—the idea aside, I can't think of any more succinct way of putting it than the above quotes do.

One God

There is one God: "*ekadhaiva anudrashtavyam*" (you should regard it as one).²⁴ Now, the Hindu creed also has a plurality of gods but the notion of a Supreme Being symbolizing Ultimate Reality is constantly put forth in The Upanishads. And this thought of unity, of non-duality ("advaitya") is at the center of Indian thought and, further, in Perennial Thought. It's like the notion of a mountain only being able to have *one* peak.

Spirit

The individual soul is a part of the all-soul. Âtman is part of Brahman. This The Upanishads teaches us. Âtman, The True Self, is the essence of the individual:

> *avinâshi tu tad viddhi yena sarvam idam tatam*
> *vinâsham avyayasyâsya na kashcit kartum arhati*
> Know that this by whom [by Âtman] this entire [body] is ingrained, is indestructible.
> No one can destroy the indestructible spirit.²⁵

---

[20] Katha Upanishad II.22.

[21] BhG XVIII.20.

[22] Shvetashvatâra Upanishad VI.11.

[23] BhG XIII.28.

[24] Brihadâranyaka Upanishad IX.4.20.

[25] BhG II.17.

In other words, The Spirit is immortal, "it doesn't die when the physical body dies" (*Na hanyate hanyamâne sharîre*).[26]

We will all live on for eternity, as part of the Eternal Light. In BhG II.12 Krishna says: "I have never not-existed, neither have you nor these princes, and we shall not cease to exist in the future":

*na tv evâham jâtu nâsam na tvam neme janâdhipâh
na caiva na bhavishyâmah sarve vayam atah param*

Ideas of the eternal quality of the essence of man, of his True Self, will come to the fore in the new era we're heading for, the Sat Yuga of truth. In all courtesy I say, acknowledge this aspect of reality, give room for it and join me in the Light.

---

[26] BhG II.20.

12. STEINER'S CHRISTOLOGY

BORDERLINE IS ABOUt the inner reality, about ideas of the esoteric strains in man and nature. *Eso-* is Greek and means "inner". And a centerpiece of western esotericism is *Christianity*. My approach to this complex of thought will here be effected with the aid of Rudolf Steiner (1861-1925). Steiner's Christology is the subject of this and the following chapter.

Rudolf Steiner elaborates on the specificity of Jesus Christ in the study *Das Johannes-Evangelium*, a series of twelve lectures from 1908 compiled in a book. I've read the Swedish version *Johannesevangeliet* (1959) and the quotes below are translated into English by me; therefore there are no pages specified. But there's also a proper English version available,[27] as *The Gospel of St. John*. In this dissertation Steiner gives his version on the uniqueness of Christ, of the specificity of his life and thought.

Below I'll note some of the traits I find fruitful in Steiner's work in question. Steiner made a lot of bold statements and I can't say that I endorse them all. But overall he makes sense, he gives Christianity a sorely needed esoteric foundation. Along with Gnosticism and

---

[27] For example online at www.rsarchive.org

Esoteric Symbolism ("Plotinism") Steiner interprets The Christian Text in a way that makes it compatible with Perennialism, more so than the parochial version given in established, official Christian thought.

Logos

Where to start, then, when looking at the Christology of Steiner? I'd say—at the beginning. As I've already intimated in chapter ten Steiner in *Das Johannes-Evangelium* says this about the origin of all: *In the beginning was Logos, whose name is I AM.* This, in itself, is one fine postulate, but I'll complement it with one of my hobbyhorses in this respect. For as I've also shown in chapter ten, before this (following Agerskov) there was Thought and Will, Light and Dark. These four factors existed in the beginning. And Thought and Will met (somehow) and became one being. And this being strove for the Light, not the Dark. And when the Light had been reached "I Am" sung out over this act as a self-confirming dictum. In this way, I maintain, Logos/God was created in the beginning. Admittedly, maybe Logos was more primeval than God, maybe Logos was "The Primeval Thought". I actually don't know, but further research may clarify this. For the time being I will go with the above scenario.

This is the meaning of the I Am-saying, a dictum that plays a central role in Steiner's thought. "I Am" is the name of Logos— and Logos is the Word, the Word eventually becoming flesh in the form of Jesus Christ. In the Biblical Gospel of John is mentioned a bit obscurely "the name of Christ". No one but Steiner has stated that this *name* (Greek *onoma*) is the above mentioned "I Am". For instance, Christ once says to God (John 12:28): "Glorify thy name" (*doksasón sou tò onoma*). That is: glorify your "I Am"...! More on what this glorifying means later.

The Beginning

Logos, a sort of divine spirit, existed in the beginning. This, Steiner tells us, we even read in The Old Testament, Genesis 1:2: "[T]he Spirit of God was hovering over the surface of the waters." But let's concentrate on The Gospel of John here. There it says: in the beginning was the Word, and everything has been made through it. Thus the beginning of this gospel:

> In the beginning was the Word,
> and the Word was with God,
> and the Word was God.
> He was in the beginning with God.
> All things were made through Him,
> and without Him nothing was made that was made.

Thus: in the beginning "I Am" existed, in the form of Logos, The Divine Word. This Word has engendered everything there is. Nothing exists without this Word. This *I Am*, this Word, is present in both the micro and macrocosm, in both the part and the whole of the Universe.

Steiner (1959) says of this: "Logos is the highest to which the human spirit can raise itself." And through Logos everything has been created—and Logos was then manifested in Jesus Christ: "And the Word became flesh." (John 1:14). Steiner also writes: "a being of highest spiritual dignity was embodied in Jesus". This is what is commonly called "the Divinely Incarnated Word of Christ". Even mainstream Christianity teaches this, although they differ from Steiner in many other respects.

The Spirit of God, existing in the beginning, descended into Jesus at the baptism in Jordan in order to teach, rise and redeem humanity—redeem *humanity as a whole*. I will get back to this in chapter thirteen, and for now I'll just say: as individuals we still have to process our karmic luggage but as a whole Jesus "saved" humanity. This is the specific Steinerian creed as we shall see, as such an integration of East and West in bringing the concept of *karma* along in the Christian narrative. Karma is the idea of cause and effect applied morally and with reincarnation as vehicle. The karmic idea for its part isn't totally alien to Western man, we already have it in sayings like "as you sow, so shall you reap" and "sin punishes itself," and in sayings by Jesus himself such as, "don't judge so that you won't be judged" (Matthew 7:1), "blessed are the meek for they shall inherit the world" (Matthew 5:5) and in Old Testament sayings like, "send your grain across the seas, and in time, profits will flow back to you" (Ecclesiastes 11:1).

Logos Lives On

Logos was embodied in Jesus Christ. Before that, it had been embodied in Adam, the first man. Steiner here refers to The Gospel of Luke. This text namely derives the genealogy of Jesus to Adam and God, and this has to be taken literally, as Steiner means. Because, in the beginning was Logos. And this was eventually embodied in Adam, then in Jesus Christ. Christ was the rebirth of God in man.

~

Logos. This is indeed a remarkable phenomenon. Again, everything has been created through this, everything lives because of it. This is what Steiner means and the beginning of The Gospel of John says it: "All things were made through Him, / and without Him nothing was made that was made."

Logos is within us all. In line with this Steiner, in *Das Johannes-Evangelium*, says that a man's body looks the way it looks due to Logos. Logos is the template of man. As mentioned, the name of Logos is "I Am"—and to say this, self-consciously saying "I Am," distinguishes man from for example the animals.

Why? Because man can speak. Animals can't. Steiner says that the ability to speak first rested with God; maybe Steiner means that God said, "I Am" when he was created, when Will was united with Thought. Then, Steiner says, God created beings who would, like him, be able to talk. This gives some clue to the specificity of Logos, its creative powers, how we exist because of Logos. The Steinerian train of thought is that the physical human body comes from Logos or The Word. The body would be able to speak, become a witness of Logos. The Word is the basis of the plan according to which we are created. The human body was built by The Word, from the beginning ordered by it so that The Word could emanate from it.

∼

"I Am"—Moses heard God saying this when God appeared before him in the burning bush (Genesis 3:14). In full God's saying went: "I Am Who I Am." In Latin this is, "Ego Sum Qui Sum." Moses became a prophet, designated by the Egyptians. According to Steiner Moses would proclaim the God who forms the embodied "I Am".

When God says "I am 'I AM'" something marvelous happens. Steiner says this "foreshadows that which Jesus Christ would bring into the world. We hear the name of Logos, we hear him already now shout to Moses: "I am, 'I Am!'" The entity shouting its name is later incarnated as *Christ Jesus, the embodied Logos.*"

Template

The template of the body is Logos. And since the beginning Logos has been active in this body. And it still is. When for example a man sleeps, when astral and mental body plus the Self is out flying on the wings of a dream, the physical body along with its ethereal body is kept alive by the presence of Logos. It's like when the PRAM battery of a computer keeps the clock and other systems going even though the computer itself is shut off.

Throughout its earthly existence, the human body has been kept alive by Logos. Man lived because Logos has been alive in his physical body, ethereal body and astral body. Along with this we also have the Self a.k.a. the True Self, the Spiritual Self or "der Atem-Selbst" as Steiner calls it, the force that makes man esoteric and intuitive, to what he essentially "is". The soul/astral body, for its part, is more flippant, it can both delve in sublime realms or be down partying in the material realm. With the Self man was able to stand independent even from Logos itself, having freedom to see life as if from the outside. Thereby the risk of indulging in materialism arose, the risk of a God-free existence. But this was useful as a challenge and a means of spiritual development.

To sum up the role of Logos in man: the light of Logos lives in the astral body. In the material ignorance of man's current mindset the light shines in. "And the meaning of life is that man shall overcome his inner darkness and get to know the Logos light."[28]

Subtle Bodies

I will soon go on elaborating on Christ as Logos etc. But first this, a more thorough background as for Steiner's just mentioned model of "the subtle bodies" (ethereal body, astral body etc). We all have a physical body. This is subtly enclosed by *the etheric body*, keeping it alive. On the next ontological level we have *the astral body*, "the soul," a volatile entity both being able to be raised to spiritual, divine levels and being dragged down into materialism, of being enmeshed by the reality of the physical body.

As for the next level Steiner doesn't expressly mention *the mental body* but others do. Like the astral body the essence of the mental body is volatile, being both able to indulge in simpler, conditioned activities like planning the everyday of its person, and more complex such as elaborating on mathematical problems. Above all these we have *the Self*, the Spirit, Âtman or even Paramâtman, "der Atem-Selbst" as intimated above.

---

[28] Steiner.

Solar Angel

Several religions worship a Sun Spirit, an elevated Solar Angel. According to Steiner the same sun spirit lives in Christ.

Steiner believes that what Zarathustra saw in the solar Deva Ahura Mazda, and the Hindus in Vishvakarman, and Moses in the burning bush (Exodus 3: 1-22) and in the fire on Mount Sinai—all this was manifestations of what ultimately became incarnate in human form in Jesus Christ.

The truly divine "I am the light of the world" (John 8:12), earlier said by the sun Devas Vishvakarman and Ahura Mazda, is now said by Jesus Christ. This Steinerian perspective is truly original, a fresh interpretation of the nature of Christ footed in other traditional documents. The specificity of Christ is highlighted by this sun Deva perspective.

Spirit of the Sun

If Christ is a sun god, then he can be seen as the essence of sunlight.

Like this: just as a human being has a soul, just as a human being has spiritual qualities, so it is with sunlight. In this respect Logos can be said to be the soul of sunlight. Thus spiritual love streams down to earth from the sun. And as people, with the I Am-affidavit integrated in us, we can receive, cherish and reciprocate this love.

An enigmatic idea Steiner gives in this context is the following. *The Elohim* are the primeval existences of Genesis (the Hebrew original of verse 1:1 says that, "in the beginning The Elohim created heaven and earth"). Steiner says: these Elohim were six solar Devas. And through the sun they still let their love powers flow. A final, seventh Eloha went to the moon and became Jehovah, the supreme God of The Old Testament. From the moon he let Truth flow down to Earth to prepare for Compassion, eventually embodied by Christ.

There is more to say about the sun's spiritual power. Once upon a time, according to Steiner's cosmology, man was manifested materially, he became a physical being. But also the divine, the Logos, must be manifested thus, "become flesh". This occurred when the forces of the six Elohim were embodied in Jesus Christ. You could say: the internal power of the sun got external shape on earth as a man. *Ecce homo*—see the man, John the Baptist said. Maybe he meant *à la* Steiner: this is the reborn divine spirit of mankind.

The physical realm: Christ is descended into this, the Son of Man thus being shut off from the deity. Once in the physical he forgets God. Then he "un-forgets" it (he is reminded) or gets an *anamnesis*, a Platonic recollection of his divine nature. He will again be aware of the spiritual. He gazes inward, sees the divine and is elevated. Through the power of Christ every son of man on earth may become such an initiate.

What is "the name of Christ" the Gospels so frequently mentions? It is, as intimated above, "I am". The Word, Logos, *I Am*, is the name of Christ. And Christ enlivened this I Am, among other things, by saying, "I am the light of the world". With such statements Christ gave humanity an impulse, he kicked the evolution to a higher plane. This "the light of the world" concept is all about the sun. It is, according to Steiner, "the sunlight that streams down to earth as Logos Power".

Christ and Identity

Hereby something about the metaphysical significance of Christ, applicable in ethical terms. This is how we defeat death and develop a pious, non-egoistic feeling of the Self.

Christ was "free from sin": he had no part in the fall, he was not materially imbued. He was karmically independent—but he went to the land of the dead and cleaned the collective human karma debt, our collective "sins".

You could say: Christ, being innocent, underwent death to defeat it, to show the illusory nature of death.

Steiner also puts a lot of significance to the crucifixion and the stream of blood pouring from the wound in the side, given by a Roman guard ("coup de lance", q.v. John 19:34). Steiner means that the blood stream from the wound of Christ "has a cosmic significance, in that it gives the earth the force necessary for evolution to continue" (Steiner in *Das Johannes-Evangelium*). And this evolution is man's spiritual development, no "Darwinian evolution" if you thought so. Steiner refers to the development of the soul and its refining through reincarnation.

The death of Christ, his defeating of death, and the significance of this for the improvement of the human ego—on this Steiner elaborates in *Das Johannes-Evangelium*. And he says that man in the beginning was a spiritual being. Then he entered into solidification, materialization and physical manifestation. Thus, he also encountered the phenomenon of physical death. Death entered the human existence and seemingly separated her from the spiritual world. Man received an independent "I", apparently rendering him into a being alone in the Cosmos.

Further, Steiner says that the physical manifestation of the Self is the blood. And here Christ enters the picture. For when, at Calvary, blood flowed from Christ's wounds, then was expelled the force that leads to increased selfishness. The unhealthy, unnecessary egoism was defeated symbolically by the blood-flow of *coup de lance*. The blood of Christ was shed—and when the blood united with the earth the aura of the planet began to shine, it began to shimmer with new colors.

The development of the Self: this is Christ's goal. Specifically, that every man should develop his "I" (his spirit, his True Self, his "Atem-Selbst") within itself. And for this there is no need for explicit trance, no initiation into a secret society, no guru. It's enough to say "I Am" and receive the Christ Impulse.

The Christ Impulse is a Steinerian concept, meaning something like "the mystery of Christ, the specificity of Christ, the special power emanating from Christ in what he said and did".

For instance, when Paul saw Christ in Damascus he observed a special light that hadn't existed before, an unmistakable light over the neighborhood. Here Paul was literally reached by the Christ impulse. To, in one way or another, embrace Christ—symbolically, intellectually, spiritually—is to become aware of the effects of the Christ Impulse.[29]

~

The Self, that which says "I Am," is one with God.

~

Christ reveals the true nature of the Father: eternal life veiled by temporary death.

~

In Christ lives the highest Solar Entity, the one in which all the Selfs have their origin.

---

[29] As for the Conversion of Paul it's to be found in Acts 9:3-9, in Galatians 1:11-16 and in 1 Corinthians 15:3-8.

Etheric Body

Hereby some more aspects of the ontological role of Christ. Now *the etheric body* is in focus.

According to Steiner Christ gave new life to man's etheric body. This allowed man's physical body to be transformed and preserved from decay and degeneration. Life could continue to thrive in the chain of reincarnation, with the physical body as an instrument.

This Steiner associates with the saying of Christ on the cross: "It is finished." (John 19:30) With this, Christ reportedly means that the dark princes of Lucifer and Ahriman were excluded from the body of Jesus. And now—the idea is—we as humans can do the same thing by receiving the Christ impulse, raise ourselves and be mentally ready.

~

According to Steiner, Logos in the form of Christ entered Jesus' body in the baptism of Jordan. For more on this, see the section "From Jesus to Christ" below. Now I'll say this about these two, still in the subject of the Etheric Body. *Jesus'* etheric body had been transformed by *Christ* so that it also could give the physical body new life. Christ's new etheric body is revealed in the words of John:

> "Father, glorify your name." Then a voice came from heaven, saying: "I have both glorified it, and will glorify it again."[30]

The verb "glorify" is in Greek *doxason*. And the noun *doxa* means opinion, judgment, reputation and appreciation, and—most importantly here—honor, glory and splendor.

Coup de Lance

Hereby something about how the earth changed because of the crucifixion. It's a complex ontology but worth studying. This, for

---

[30] John 12:28.

instance, can be seen as the ontological background of Joseph Plunkett's poem,

> I see his blood upon the rose,
> his face is every flower,
> his cross is every tree.

Jesus Christ has an all-pervading nature. In *Das Johannes-Evangelium* Steiner says: earth's aura changes when the blood of Christ flows from the wound he had received from the lance. Earth's astral and etheric body changes when the blood unites with the earth. Then, namely,

> the force, the impulse, which could only flow from the sun to the earth, began to unite with the earth itself. And because the Logos began to unite with earth, thereby the aura of the earth was changed.

If so, Christ is the spirit of the earth for as Steiner writes: "Christ is the spirit of the earth, the earth is his body."

Steiner also means that the power of Christ heals—it exists in the earth, imbued with Christ's essence, with the Logos. "Christ as the Earth Spirit flows through our body." I'm not saying that this expressly is the case but it's an intriguing theory. Was the blood of Christ, uniting with the earth, necessary for evolution to proceed, for life to continue developing on earth? This is what Steiner means.

Septenaries

There are several *septenaries* in The Gospel of John. Like the seven wonders performed by Christ (transforming water to wine etc), his seven walks to Judaea, seven speeches by Christ and seven witnesses of the divinity of Christ. Here I'll just look closer on one such septenary, the seven "I Am"-sayings by Christ, since "I Am" plays some role in the ethical outline I make in chapter fourteen of this study, *Borderline*.

These are the seven "I Am's" in The Gospel of John: I am the bread of life, I am the light of the world, I am the way, the truth and the life, I am the door into the sheep, I am the good shepherd, I am the resurrection and the life, I am the true vine.

From Jesus to Christ

The Gospel of John, the eleventh chapter, is about Lazarus. Until this chapter Christ gradually develops the physical, etheric and astral body he inherited from Jesus. And on the cross, it is finished: matter has been overcome, full incarnation is reached and death has been defeated.

Thus, Jesus and Christ are distinct entities from the outset. When Jesus is 30 his Self departs to prepare a place for Christ. It takes place during the baptism in the Jordan river. The Solar Deva Christ takes possession of Jesus' physical body, etheric body and astral body. Jesus, for his part, had previous incarnations. But the Christ being had never previously incarnated in a physical body. It needed a highly developed human tool and got it in Jesus.

All this is according to Steiner in *Das Johannes-Evangelium*. With a modern term Christ is a *walk-in* in Jesus.

Jesus received Christ. Steiner here refers to Luke 2:57 where it's said that Jesus developed his astral body (wisdom), and the etheric body (figure), in order to receive Christ. And "physical beauty" in this context was how the physical body reflected all this.

Reborn Divine Spirit

In Christ a divine self was manifested. The god that was in Adam now appeared again. And (says Steiner), in the Holy Grail this higher divine self survives, a stage to which every man can raise himself by willpower.

The Word became flesh: this can be described as "the rebirth of God in man." The universal human Self was reborn, the spirit of God revitalizing man. Put another way: this was completed as a prerequisite for the rebirth of each person's higher self.

Christ is humanity's reborn divine spirit.

I Am

Lucifer plays some role in Steiner's thought. As for the Steinerian Christology this can be said in the context. Christ transformed Lucifer's gifts *freedom* and *independence* to *love*. And in unity with Christ, we are led to spiritual love.

Lucifer's freedom strain, Steiner says, is necessary for humanity to absorb. This freedom breaks the ties of blood and herd mentality, the tribal mindset.

With all due respect to ethnic identity and the right to belong to a people, it can be said: in olden times blood ties ruled supreme, such as blood-related weddings and blood-based love relationships. Today, we still have the right to preserve our respective ethnic heritages, like marrying within our own racial group. But along with this a more spiritual element is also present now. The individual's own development and Will to Power is part of the process. According to Steiner Lucifer has some part in this. His freedom doctrine has received clearance. But note: without the love doctrine of Christ we would only have egotism, devoid of compassion.

~

Man lives on earth to become fully conscious, to achieve his I Am-nature. According to Steiner it can be understood as "God is, and I in him." Christ is the one that provides the impetus for this. And in days of old the Bible only advocated tribal and group mentality, a blood relation to "Father Abraham". Along with Christ came the idea of a spiritual fatherhood, the essence of the spiritual, esoteric paradigm.

Steiner interprets Christ's relation to Abraham like this: "Before Abraham was, I AM existed. I and the Father are one!" [Freely after John 8:58]

As for esoteric Christianity teaching "God is me, I am him," this is the same idea that Veda philosophy teaches: Âtman is in Brahman, Brahman is in Âtman. (For Veda philosophy specifically, see chapter eleven of *Borderline*.)

Mankind's Spiritual Development

Throughout all of his teachings Steiner held a grand view of mankind and its spiritual development. In olden times he imagined that we lived on the continent of Atlantis where intuition and clear seeing was abounding. Since then man has developed into a brainy, self-aware, intellectually disposed, discursively thinking creature separated from God. But now, with the spiritual resurgence originating with such luminaries as Manu, Buddha, Orpheus and Christ and more recent figures like Steiner, Jung and Nietzsche, the Atlantic lucidity can be regained, now united with individual self-consciousness and rationality.

The old, spiritually clear-sighted, intuitive mindset associated with Atlantis, is to be united with the modern, god-separated, individual, rational development of mankind. In their integration man will be taken to the next step in the evolution. In other words, the new paradigm will not be a total negation of the rationalistic, nihilistic, egoistic era but an encompassing of it, within a holistic framework. And this is the integral esotericism I've intimated in this book, of unifying reason with intuition and tradition with modernity.

13. FURTHER INQUIRIES INTO STEINER'S CHRISTOLOGY

H<small>EREBY SOME MORE</small> elaborations on Rudolf Steiner's Christology. As before I don't preach this as gospel truth in every word, but on the whole I see these ideas as clarifying—from a perspective of western and eastern spirituality and from a perspective of esoteric thought in general. The common strain of Christian thought to me seems devoid of esotericism, compensated with ritualism and a focus on the historical nature of Christ. This negligence of esotericism can be seen in St Paul's advocating of "faith alone," only this will guide us, and to seek further answers is seen as "Gnostic" and worthy of contempt. Steiner, in contrast to this, gives Christianity a much needed metaphysical interpretation.

Carlgren

I've read Frans Carlgren's *Den antroposofiska kunskapsvägen* (*The Anthroposophic Way of Knowledge*, 1980). There we get some perspectives on Steiner's Christology. I will illustrate the topical ideas of that book in the form of questions and answers. Partly this will become a repetition of what I said in the previous chapter. The translations below into English are made by me.

Q: How did Christ vitalize humanity?
A: Carlgren: "By coming in touch with Christ's own life forces, with the unique etheric force field that was formed in that he lived and died in a human body. (...) From The Risen Christ emanates new life to all mankind, and through it every human—if he so wishes"—can transform himself and rise to the Logos-archetype that Christ embodied.

Q: After Calvary, where did Christ's physical body go?
A: It was taken up by the earthquake mentioned in Matthew 27:51. The sarcophagus and the shroud were still there, as the Gospels testify to.

Q: How did Christ transform Jesus' body?
A: He gave his subtle bodies a superhuman structure. And after death, his etheric force field showed up in almost physical form. Through the ages, after his death and resurrection, many people have "seen Christ". And it seemingly works like this: when Christ after death was released from his physical body he could have let the etheric body dissolve—but he kept it alive, perpetuated it in human form so that he (although he essentially had ascended to higher spheres) "seemed human". This showed how you can conquer death, it shows "the power of mind over matter". Among other things.

Q: What was Christ's mission on earth?
A: Ontologically he had the task of revitalizing the human etheric body. At this time—"Year Zero"—namely, man's etheric body had become too attached to the physical body. Thus was our post-mortem consciousness weakened. See here the classical Greek Hades visions, like Odysseus' journey to the underworld where he meets a longing Achilles, wishing rather

to be a beggar on earth than king in the land of shadows: there is no hope beyond the grave, all is darkness and emptiness...! But even after death man has the need of a spiritual, conscious life. In order to promote our development and reconnecting us to Heaven, divine powers arranged to send us a message in the form of Jesus Christ, the Spirit of God in human form. "God became human".

Q: In what way is the presence of Christ discernible in pre-Christian texts?
A: See, for example, how the Sumerian divinity Inanna/Ishtar is tormented for three days, dies and is resurrected. This cycle is in some way also reflected in the legends of Osiris, Adonis, Apis, Ahura Mazda, Apollo, Balder and Odin. And all of these can be seen as fragmented premonitions of the way Christ took, Steiner says.

In the context of this, see also Apuleius in the text *Proserpina Mystery*: "In the night I saw the sun shine brightly." And *The Messianic Eclogue* of Virgil, as well as the Jewish Messiah movement, in some way related to Jewish Eschatology (q.v. Isaiah, Ezekiel, Zechariah etc.). Reportedly, "to see the sun at midnight" is the mystical concept for this pre-Christ syndrome.

Q: How is the solar nature of Christ shown in the Bible?
A: Among other things, in Jesus' statement in Matthew 17: 1-8, when full control of the etheric body is achieved. The Solar Being in question is also shown in the mighty angel appearing in Revelation 1: 13-19. And (as we saw in the previous chapter), in The Gospel of John, in the saying "I am the light of the world". And in The Gospel of Matthew, chapter seventeen, when Jesus is transformed into a Being of Light before the eyes of Peter, James and John (a.k.a. "The Transfiguration"). Apart from the Bible, the solar nature of Christ appears in near-death experiences in modern times when people have seen a Being of Light.

Q: After Christ's death and his spiritual journey to the land of the dead (with its enlightening outreach, the process "[t]o give light to them that sit in darkness and in the shadow of death"; Luke 1:79), what happened?
A: On the dawn of Easter Sunday the Spirit of Christ appeared on earth, after having flowed Hades with light and hope.

Q: Suppose that Christ became Earth's spirit after *Coup de Lance*. What happened next; what says Steiner on the Logos force after Calvary?
A: "Ever since the incident at Calvary the earth spiritually contains that power within himself which will again bring it together the with the sun." Into the earth was absorbed "the Solar Logos Power of Calvary directly, through the blood of Jesus", thus, now lives in the earth—in the ground and in all the plants and animals, indeed, in all of us—"Logos himself who through Golgotha became the spirit of the earth."

Q: The Gospels in relating the legend of the Crucifixion, speaking of how "the earth trembled," "the sun lost its light" and "the veil was rent," should these be understood literally?
A: According to Steiner, yes.

Q: The physical human body is the abode of the Spirit Self, "der Atem-Selbst". Is it the same with the sun and the sunlight, are these tangible vessels for something spiritual?
A: Yes. The spirit of the sun is Logos-Christ.

Secret Knowledge

Finally, in this Christological subtheme, I'll take a brief look at a book by Rudolf Steiner that adds some clues to his views on Christ. The title is *Grunddragen av vetenskapen om det fördolda* (German, *Die Geheimwissenschaft im Umriss*, 1910). The Q and A pattern from above is retained.

Q: What happened to Christ in his moment of death?
A: When Christ died he poured out his being in the aura of the earth. Thus, humanity—if it wants—can become a part of the spiritual forces that were gathered in Christ's essence.

Q: How does The Christ Impulse affect man's state between death and life?
A: The Calvary Event enables a man to bring his earthly experience to heaven. There isn't any longer the negative force of Ahriman around to put a veil over man's outlook in this World Beyond the Beyond, for this Ahriman was defeated by Christ's deeds, through the enlightening activities of Christ in Hades between his death on the cross and the resurrection.

Christ intervened on behalf of man. After living in the everyday world and experiencing the death of its physical body, an individual soul now can go unimpeded to heaven for karmic debrief, and then without hindrance move on to the next earthly existence, the individual's next life, a new life in *samsâra* with the goal of continued spiritual evolution and development.

Q: How can Trinity be expressed geometrically?
A: The Father is the center, the Son is the surface and the Spirit is the radius, i.e., the distance from the surface to the center.

Q. In the previous chapter of this book, *Borderline*, there was mentioned how Christ abolished humanity's collective karmic debt. Can you elaborate on Steiner's idea of this?
A: According to Steiner in *Die Geheimwissenschaft im Umriss*, the role of Christ erasing our collective karma is seen in John 8 where he "writes on the ground" while a sinner is accused. The karmic justice, according to Steiner, remains valid by being "written in the earth," the earth whose spirit Christ is (or will become after Calvary)—but the overall, collective effect of karma Christ takes on himself so as not the continued development of the world and mankind suffers.

In other words, Christ takes away the objective effects of an individual's deeds: the collective debt is wiped out. But the individual's subjective karma remains.

One can also say: individual man redeems himself by his personal karmic exertions, while Christ redeems mankind and the earth as a whole.

Q: Elaborate.
A: Indeed I will. In Steinerian and Christian terms "the original sin" is abolished by Christ's death on the cross. By this the world's overall evolutionary debt was written off by him. Then, by referring to Christ, an individual may acknowledge that Christ lives in him in the form of Logos; this Logos has "redeemed" the world while the individual's personal redemption obeys the law of karma.

Q: You say that man's individual karma remains to be worked off and payed off. But I've heard that every man's karmic dept as of now, in the 2010s, is abolished. Karma and reincarnation are history from now on, by Kâli Yuga giving way to Sat Yuga or some-such. The current lives we live will be our last steps in *samsâra*. Of course if someone dearly wishes to be incarnated again that may be granted. But overall samsâra, in the form of "tedious trudging through life after life in the physical realm," is reaching its very end in this very age.
A: That may be so. I'm not gifted with second sight, I'm no spiritual know-it-all. So I'll stick to topic, the mission of Christ in general and how he changed man's plight after death. According to Steiner it can be summarized as: in the Christian reality, after death we now could all go to "Heaven" for a recapitulation of our earthly life. This we could do thanks to Christ; we were not longer trapped in a Hadean shadow existence. By this development we were additionally able to do this: by way of reincarnation bringing with us or past experiences to the next life, plus the spiritual influences we got from this heavenly séjour. Thus Steiner's view of man's journey through samsâra and the role of Christ in it.

14. HOLISTIC ETHICS: SOME NOTES

As stated in the Introduction I adhere to the Primordial Tradition. The basic element of my Perennial creed is: God is the Primeval Light, and as individuals we are parts of that Light. The world as a whole is harmonious, ordered and beautiful. Presupposing this, what kind of ethic would this engender? What "ought" can be derived from this "is"?

You could say: I'm no card-carrying teacher of philosophy. I'm merely an amateur—an amateur interested in sketching a comprehensive outlook for these times. And part of that outlook is the following moral deliberations. I here outline an ethic for these times, an ethic with some spiritual foundations. Below I will discuss how such an ethic might look, based on the holistic paradigm sketched in this book. The concepts I discuss first are *compassion*, *truth* and *willpower*. Then I'll move on to elements like *holism*, *here-and-now* and *"I Am"*.

To Be Good

Any ethic must deal with "how to be good". Conversely, you can't strike goodness, kindness, compassion etc. out of ethics. T. S. Eliot, for his part, contemptuously spoke about "dreaming of systems so perfect that no one will need to be good".[31] This is worth considering. At the same time it's hard to say, "this is an ethic teaching you how to be good". An ethic on how to be good has to be created by a good man. And it's hard to make such a claim, that of being a good man. "No one is good except God alone," Jesus says in Mark 10:18.

You see: not even Jesus expressly said that he was good. Because, only God is good. However, Jesus did say, "I Am". That is the core sentence of all philosophy and I will return to it later in this chapter.

Compassion

No one but God is essentially good. This we can remember. This is a memento for dualistic minds, those thinking, "either you're good or you're not". The tendency to find fault with persons, and then, seeing that—for instance—Jesus also had a fierce side, prophesying war, ("I have not come to bring peace, but a sword," Matthew 10:34)—then all of his philosophy has to discarded.

That kind of dualism I don't endorse, the attitude of "either 100% for or 100% against". Instead, in the current context goodness and compassion should be held as *ideals to strive* for. Compassion is a constant lodestar for the ethically disposed person.

And for the rigorous, "modern" man who thinks that compassion has no place in this world, that it's outdated, I'd say: at least, you have to have compassion with yourself. Do you have that? Are you giving yourself a pat on the shoulder now and then? Or are you driving yourself ever on to this and that goal? This will end in disaster. You have to cut some slack, even towards yourself. That's the beginning of getting to know compassion. "Charity starts at home." And: "Love thy neighbor *as thyself*." The last part, the "thyself" part, is fundamental to everything. You have a duty to love yourself.

---

31 "Choruses from The Rock", 1934.

A specific aspect of "loving yourself" was given by Simone Weil. She said that "God loves himself *through* us," meaning that he is the Primeval Light acknowledging every single individual Light of the creation. As individuals, we have to let that force acknowledge itself in us.

That's the first element of my ethical system. Acknowledge compassion, at least in the form of appreciating yourself. Expressed in a more esoteric, symbolic fashion, you could say: "acknowledge the Rose Flame". According to esoteric theory we have a Threefold Flame in our hearts. It's made up of the Rose Flame, symbolizing *Compassion*, a Yellow Flame symbolizing *Truth*, and a Blue Flame symbolizing *God*. This can give us a pattern for the rest of this ethical discussion.

Truth

As for the second part of my ethical outline, along with Compassion, we have *Truth*. The prime mental activity of a man should be "to seek truth, speak truth". Again, we mustn't see dualistically on this ("either you're truthful or you're not"). Truth is an ideal to strive for. Should we be caught lying we aren't eternally doomed, we've just strayed from the path.

Will

Now I've mentioned Compassion and Truth. The third element of this ethical troika is associated with God. I'm talking about *Will*. And Willpower is truly a neglected force in ethics.

Willpower is a core concept having come into some sort of disrepute. Either it's linked to a certain ideology blooming for over seventy years ago in Europe, by today's pundits associated with chauvinism and illegality, or it's confused with *desire*, as in

Schopenhauer's thought. But there's another way of looking at willpower, a way with some traditional footing. For in a Gnostic gospel it says, "Will doesn't make them into sinners, but lack of will does."[32] This intimates the spiritual nature of will. *Willpower* is pure and idealistic; contrariwise, *desire* is directed toward materialism, toward indulging in food, drink and sex. Will is always good. "Good will" thus is a sort of tautology; contrariwise, there is no evil will. This the French philosopher Alain said. "Alain" was the alias of Émile Chartier (1868-1951).

As we saw in chapter 10, Will and Light are primeval forces. Esotericism already knows this. Now it's time for ethics to acknowledge the same basic tenet. Pure will is divine.

⁓

We all have willpower. We just need to discover it, acknowledge it. First and foremost, you can exercise will over yourself. This is the paramount use of "the Will to Power" that Nietzsche spoke of. Realize your inner will, nurture it; live the will-directed life and be free. Realize all the aspects of will such as "the will to forgive," "the will to meditate," "the will to become a better person."

Will is needed both for conducting the active and the contemplative life. Will is needed both for meditation and for physical exercise. For instance, you don't start to meditate by chance. Neither do you start a physical training program by chance. Will is the prime mover in both the *vita activa* and the *vita contemplativa*.

Will is needed for an individual to assume responsibility in his life. Carlos Castaneda for his part had *assuming responsibility* as one of the core concepts of his creed and in essence this is an aspect of willpower. As individuals we have to take charge over our lives. This is the only way. If you don't you'll become the slave of some master, whether IRL or virtually. We have to assume responsibility for whom we are, as spiritual individuals, as soul-endowed persons— and as citizens partaking in society, debating freely, spreading new, old and new-old ways of thinking, challenging the consensus.

---

[32] The Gospel of Philip, verse 64.

Realize your will. Thus you will live a strong, active, responsible and free life. As for how freedom and responsibility are linked, listen to what Robert A. Heinlein said in *The Moon Is A Harsh Mistress,* a novel from 1966: "I am free because I know that I alone am morally responsible for everything I do."

Taking Control

Willpower for the individual primarily means this: to take control over your inner mind, over thought. For the contemplative mood this means: the wavering thoughts are reined in and put to rest, helping you to relax. For the active mood this means: the disparate thoughts are systematized and directed toward a common goal, an operational endeavor.

A conscious individual takes control of every thought, every emotion, every mental activity going on inside him. This is "the Will to Power over Oneself". An esotericist is the master of himself thanks to putting Willpower to the fore.

A conscious operator can always make "a short halt," assess the situation at hand and ask himself: now I'm reacting to this situation with feeling "X"; do I really want this? For example: the individual lies in bed trying to sleep, worrying about a visit to the dentist the next day. With his willpower mustered he can put the indulging thoughts to rest and think, "We'll cross that bridge when we get to it, now it's night, now I'll sleep."

Again: assume responsibility for whom you are. Julius Evola once said (in *Ride the Tiger*) that we are not "thrown out" in this world, German "geworfen" as Heidegger put it. Instead, we are who we are according to eternal spiritual laws (karma, the law of cause and effect, having our deeds and actions in a previous life affect the person we are now). So I'd say: vindicating "Geworfenheit", and the akin idea of humans as "being *condemned* to freedom" (q.v. Sartre), is "the last refuge of a scoundrel". Instead, we are who we are for a reason. So acknowledge this, muster will and live the free and active life in volitional glory.

Holism

Above I've discussed Compassion, Truth and Will within a moral framework. Now I'll broaden the ethical outlook. It's done by speaking of *Holism*, the *Here and Now*-impulse and the *I Am*-motto.

This book, *Borderline*, is based on the concept of holism. Here I'll repeat some of the basic tenets of this, giving it all an existential slant. Holism is about seeing the big picture, of having the presence of The Whole immanently with you in whatever you do or think. Conversely, a holistically minded person is not a reductionist or dyed-in-the-wool materialist.

As for the opposite of holism, reductionism, I've already treated it in chapter five. Here it will suffice to say: it's true that we might need to simplify and reduce some situations in order to get things done. If you have to clear the snow, dig a hole or fix your bike you don't get embroiled in holistic reasoning. This is the wrong way to look at tasks of this kind. But for your general outlook on life, yourself and your environment, be it social, biological and / or societal, a holistic approach is needed, especially in these times, the 2010s when the—as Jünger said—"Mauretanian" outlook is dominant, which could be described as "the principles of machine technology applied to politics". Today's politicians, academics and media messiahs all seem to have a reductionist, simplistic, mechanistic approach to things. Contrariwise, the latter-day esotericist is helped by a holistic view. For instance, he doesn't see the overall aim of society as "increasing growth," this is a typically one-eyed approach, footed in materialism; instead a contemporary esotericist sees the question of overall aims from the aspects of tradition, of impact on the societal fabric and of environmental issues.

Holism also has a bearing on spiritual areas. For instance, in looking at past cultural eras, past masters and classics of yesteryear, a studied holist would never even answer questions like, "Is antiquity good or bad, do we need it or shall we stop teaching about it?" Since the question itself is wrongly put, a question posed by a mechanistic mind, a mind demanding a yes-or-no-answer to everything. Of course antiquity has something to say to us, some aspects of it more than others, but entirely discarding of the ancient heritage is impossible.

On the esoteric, philosophic level holism is immanent. To fully grasp documents like the Bhagavad-Gîtâ, the Upanishads, the Gospels (both the canonical and the Gnostic ones) we need a holistic approach, being able to take in the possibly conflicting aspects of each document. We can't read them with a reductionist mindset, simplistically asking ourselves if this text is good or bad for contemporary humanity or for ourselves specifically.

A holist is able to integrate opposites, like Carl Jung did (q.v. chapter eighteen). A true esotericist has the ability to somewhat live with contradictions. This is the mature way of relating to art, philosophy and spirituality. Life isn't strictly logical, reality isn't structured according to a reductionist, dualist, materialist mindset. Holism may be hard to live by at the outset, it hasn't got any simple formulas for grasping reality, but after a while this approach gives the esotericist the freedom and inspiration to see the world as an organism and not a mechanism—seeing the world and himself as beings functioning with part and whole inter-working and not as serially working machines.

Here and Now

So much, then, about Holism. The next ethical-ontological concept that I like to focus on is the attitude of Here-and-Now. It's akin to the Holistic and Willpower concepts. But I'll give it a separate headline in order to make this basic discussion more digestible.

"Here and Now: is this really spiritual?", you might ask. For instance, we've heard about people saying, "live as if there's no tomorrow, live life to the full right now". And true, the materialistic mind might interpret everything in a deranged way. But for the spiritually minded operator, the Aristocrat of the Soul, *Here and Now* is about being able to focus his whole being on the moment at hand. He discards the common "doing it tomorrow," "someone else will do it" approach. Instead he assumes responsibility for living in the now and gets going immediately. In a more subtle way it's about being able to exercise Will at any moment, anytime, anywhere. The esotericist lives in the Now and so is able to relax and enjoy every moment, whether it's in an environment of fierce and hectic action or one of tranquility.

A true esotericist is never bored. He says to himself: "This moment right now is the best, the worst, the 'whatever' moment I've ever lived." And so he takes a deep breath, reassesses the situation and goes on living as if nothing has happened. But something has, indeed, happened: he has taken volitional control of his situation, and so everything is changed. "As we are, so we see" is a dictum that might fit my ethics *in nuce*. And the Here and Now-concept makes us see it, along with the Willpower concept.

A Core Concept

Now for a final core concept of my ethical discussion. It's a concept overwhelming in its simplicity and magnificence, and it is: *I Am*.

You could say: Truth, Compassion, Willpower, Holism and Here-and-Now are summarized in this saying, "I Am". You could also say that "everything" in ethics and ontology is embodied in the I Am-concept. It's the self-affirming formula uniting God with Man. As we saw in chapter ten I suggested the following ontological model for the creation of the world: "In the beginning Will united with Thought, then choosing Light and saying "I Am" to seal the deal, the saying itself being the birth of God as a splendid, super-real being, the beginning and end of everything."

In other words: in the beginning God created the Universe, and was himself created, by saying "I AM"—and when we, as human beings say the same, we become united with God.

By saying "I Am" we become witnesses of Logos, whose name is "I Am".

I Am. My main source for lifting this concept is the above treated Steiner study, *Das Johannes-Evangelium* (q.v. chapters

12-13). Another 20th century thinker having stressed this concept is one Guy Ballard. Also, in modern channellings from diverse beings (Mother Earth, Saint Germain and other Ascended Masters) the I Am-saying is frequent, being a sort of token of identification, a sign saying that the speaker is in line with God and the Light. I'm neither a typical spiritualist, Ballardist or a Steinerist but I do confess that "I Am" and the way that Steiner has elaborated upon this has clarified my view on Christianity, giving it more ontological depth, making it appropriate for a 21st century, consciously reflecting man.

As intimated in chapter twelve, the I Am-saying can be traced to Jesus Christ. As I've already mentioned he says it seven times in the Bible, in The Gospel of John: "I am the good shepherd," "I am the door to the sheep," "I am the true vine," "I am the bread of life," "I am the way, the truth, the life," "I am the resurrection and the life" and "I am the light of the world".

Affirmation

The book you're now reading is not a Christian document. It's *Borderline*. And the I Am-saying is not about going to church and kneeling before a priest. Saying "I Am" is about affirming yourself as a spiritual being, a man with a divine element in him. As stated above, Steiner goes on to say that this I Am-concept is given also in the Old Testament, in Moses' meeting with God in the burning bush (Exodus 3). God in this scene presented himself as, "I Am That I Am," and to Steiner this is the same being stating his case that we later saw in The Gospel of John. The being saying, "I Am," is the Logos. "I Am" is the "name" of Jesus and essentially of God, the name so frequently mentioned in the New Testament ("Lord, glorify your name," "ask of it in my name," "many will come in my name" etc).

"I Am": in the beginning was Logos, whose name is, "I Am". Thus according to Steiner. And for this study, *Borderline*, this can suffice as for the theological, Christian part. The I Am saying is Christian in origin but as intimated it's also something more, something general and elementary. For example, as a dictum it's eminently succinct and simple. Anyone can say it. As for India's Vedic tradition this also has succinct sayings (like *tat tvam asi*, stating the unity between the individual Self with the Absolute) but "I Am" is indeed shorter and more concise. In Latin even more so: *Sum*.

The I Am-saying is the formula for the esotericist affirming his spiritual self. By saying "I Am" he acknowledges that he has a will, that his inner light is a fragment of the Primeval Light, the divine light. By saying "I Am" the individual becomes what he is, free and responsible at the same time.

"I Am" can be combined with any positive concept into *affirmations* in the form of simple, energizing statements. Like, "I Am Swedish," "I Am Willpower," "I Am Light," "I Am Creative" et cetera. As intimated it's hard to reduce reality into a formula, and it's equally hard to reduce a system of thought into a formula, but if you've followed me in this chapter of ethical elaborations you have to agree that the formula summing up the creed the best is—I AM.

"I Am"—I don't have an "all rights reserved" stamp on this. As I said, Steiner was the one who taught me the meaning of the concept. "I Am" is the affirmation of yourself as a moral actor, as an ethical individual taking charge of your life in a strong, assertive and spiritual fashion.

Say to yourself, "I Am," and you're ready for everything.

15. ON EQUANIMITY

How many philosophers meditate? Did Nietzsche meditate? Does the random school philosopher meditate? I can't vouch for them, but if you're engaged in *Seinsphilosophie* you have to be able to practice *volitional mental calm*. Every spiritual actor must be able to reach a state of peace, tranquility and equanimity. Having a concept of mental serenity is essential to an operational esotericist, to a thinker seeing himself as a microcosmic mirror of the macrocosm. Like Ezra Pound said: "If a man have not order within him / he can not spread order about him."

Being Calm

In the previous chapter I sketched an esotericist ethic. And central to all forms of esotericism is to calm down. An esotericist must know how to calm down. How to reach inner harmony, quieting down the internal monologue: that's the subject of this chapter. I choose to call this element of my ethical discussion "C3," standing for "calm, cool and collected".

Embracing the esotericist doctrine is to acknowledge the *inner reality* of man, the inner mind and its workings. *Eso* is Greek and means "inner". The opposite is "exo" (outer).

In homine interiore habitat veritas means "in man's inner dwells the truth." "It's decided within," as Goethe said ("Im Innern ist's getan").

The inner mind is the realm of will and thought. Will has to take control over thought. And Will-Thought, in its turn, has to control the body.

~

As I stated in the previous chapter: whether you live the *vita activa* or the *vita contemplativa* you have to have Willpower to the fore in your mindset. To meditate demands willpower; for example, you never start meditating by chance. Also, to engage in physical exercises takes willpower; for instance, you never start a training program by chance. Willpower is the key, both to equanimity and bodily action. And aspects on the expressly active life is covered in the next chapter. Here, therefore, I will say something about equanimity, esotericist style: the C3 concept.

"C3" means to be "calm, cool and collected". It's about reaching mental peace and quiet. Hereby some clues of how I personally do to calm down.

For instance, if I wake up in the middle of the night and it's too early to get up, how do I do to get back to sleep? Here it's important not to start thinking in everyday ways. You have to avoid the commonly mental approach to things. So I'd say: kill the everyday thought and instead direct it into intuitive thinking, into colors and images. As for images, I've found that is useful to return to the dream you just dreamed before this unwanted awaking. Whether it was a nightmare or a sweet dream it calms you down trying to remember the images of that dream. Also, recalling past dream images, scenes etc. of dreams you've dreamed on other nights, is useful in getting back to sleep. For this, it's a good habit to write down your dreams. Just the images, just the bare-bones symbolic features, and no attempts at interpretation. This is my kind of favorite dream book.

When waking in the middle of the night it takes willpower not to start thinking about everyday problems. Already in The Poetic Edda we see this problem highlighted: "An anxious man lies awake each night / brooding over this and that; / when morning comes the man is tired / and everything is as before."[33]

Pneuma

To calm down is not merely about getting back to sleep in the middle of the night. It's also about finding calm while you're awake.

The core phenomenon of calming down, reaching mental quiet, is about bringing the body to rest. What body function is it easiest for us to control? As intimated, it's the breath. "To control your breath" can be learned within the system of East Asian yoga (ashtanga yoga, Transcendental Meditation etc.). The symbol for this is a man sitting with legs folded and back strait, that is, in the lotus position. Personally, I'm not particularly into this kind of *âsana yoga* (sitting yoga). If my way of "relaxing systematically" even can be called yoga, I practice it lying down flat on my back on the bed. The legs should be straight. Then, the hands should either be placed flat on the bed or clasped, resting on the midsection; whatever feels most comfortable.

Anyhow, when lying thus, I try to calm down my breath. This is done by willpower. For example, in your mind you can formulate the command, "I will now calm down my breathing".

I'm no yoga teacher. But I know how to calm down using willpower. And controlling your breath is step one.

Again, I prefer lying on the bed, flat on my back, with legs straight and arms flat on the bed. You should lie relaxed but straight, not in any way curled up. Then it's about calming down the breath as above. Moreover, I've found that a very basic form of relaxing standing up can be efficient. You don't have to be in your bedroom in order to calm down. Think about it: during the day

---

[33] Havamal, verse 23.

there are many occasions when you have to wait. During all these waits, don't get upset, don't be stressed out. Everything comes to him who waits. And in the meantime, for instance, when you're standing in line, stand with equal weight distribution on both your feet, have the arms relaxed—and breathe. Not in an inflexible way, not in a forced way, but calmly and deliberately. This is a surefire way to calm down, a sort of micro yoga.

Also, sitting straight in a chair is a fine way of relaxing. Back straight, feet flat on the floor. Then try to control your breath.

That's how I "relax systematically," keeping *calm, cool and collected* throughout the day.

And that's what every esotericist has to be. Every man or woman claiming to be a traditional esotericist, in touch with Being and exerting traditional values, has to be C3. As an esotericist you have to include yourself in the overall equation—in the Cosmos, in Being, in *Sein*, in Sat. Conversely, a man that purports to teach *Seinsphilosophie*, the creed stressing harmony, beauty and order, without having a clue on how he himself can be harmonic, is an absurdity. You can't be a teacher of the way of Plotinus, Goethe, Jung and Jünger being a sardonic, nihilist cynic.

The Gita

Samatva is the Sanskrit word for "peace of mind". The direct translation is "equality," in spiritual contexts the same as "equanimity". Bhagavad-Gîtâ 2:48 says this about samatva:

> *yogasthah kuru karmâni sangam tyaktvâ dhanamjaya*
> *siddhyasiddhyoh samo bhûtvâ samatvam yoga ucyate*
> (Practice yoga, Dhanamjaya, abandon the bonds [to the material world],
> be unaffected by success or failure; this evenness of mind is called yoga).

"Yoga" is to unite the Individual Consciousness with the Absolute Consciousness, and samatva is a prerequisite for this union. A BhG quote related to this, by using the word *sama* ("equal"), is 2:14:

*mâtrasparshâs tu kaunteya shîtoshna-sukha-duhkha-dâh
âgamâpâyino 'nityâs tâms titikshasva bhârata*
(O son of Kuntî; the sensations bring pain and pleasure, hot and cold;
they are coming and going and impermanent. Endure them, Bhârata.)

The immediately following verse brings the equanimity argument home:

*yam hi na vyathayanty ete purusham purusharishabha
sama-duhkha-sukham dhîram so 'mritatvâya kalpate*
(O bull among men; they [the sensations] don't agitate the person being
equal to pleasure and pain and resolute; he's apt for immortality.)

Western Strains

Not only the ancient Hindus stressed the need for a quiet mind. We had it even in the ancient West, in the school of Stoicism. They sported the ideal of *apateia*. This, for its part, was no mere *apathy*; apathy is rather part of the Chaotic Mindset (see chapter seventeen), in the form of a mindless, nihilist indifference. *Apateia*, on the other hand, is an elevated equanimity, the ability to perform acts without being engaged, just like *samatva*. A third example of the same is the French concept of *désinvolture*, held as an ideal by Ernst Jünger. In *The Adventurous Heart* (2012) there's an essay on the subject. Désinvolture is to be interpreted as "unconcerned attitude," "elevated tranquility" or "not desirous", an attitude said to have been cherished in courts in southern medieval France. To exert désinvolture is

> to partake in life but not being engaged, with a zen Buddhist calm seeing life passing by. A subtle form of active-passive meditation, in the middle of the hubbub. With a pious

sentiment neither attaching yourself to luck or bad fortune, success or failure (...).³⁴

Thus, what I've said in this chapter may give the reader some clues on how to be "calm, cool and collected".

---

³⁴ Svensson 2014, p 129.

16. ON ACTING

IN THE TWO PRECEDING chapters I've treated some ethical aspects of holism. At the center of ethics is *the action*, how to act. Ethics teaches us how to act. And in sync with the above sketched ethics you could say the following about acting holistically: an esoteric actor acknowledges his Inner Light. In doing this he finds his way through life both by reason and intuitively, experiencing alternatives of action by trial and error, not by adhering to that or the other dogma.

Having to Act

The basic tenet of "how to act" is this: we *have* to act. No man can totally abstain from acting. This is what we read in Bhagavad-Gîtâ 3:5 a-b and 3:8 c-d:

> *na hi kashcit kshanam api jâtu tishthaty akarma-krit (...)*
> *sharîra-yâtrâpi ca te na prasiddhyed akarmanah*
> (No one can, not even for an instant, remain wholly passive. (...) You can't sustain your body without working.)

In order to stay alive and feed your body you have to work. And even if you're a quietist, fasting and sitting meditating, you have to *breathe*. Breathing too is an action, this too is an operation you have to perform as a living creature.

Breathing and meditation were covered in the previous chapter. This chapter is about how a certain form of action leads to a higher form of meditation. It's about gaining a sense of rest, a glorified state of calm, while acting.

The active side of Borderline ethics is, you could say, the *l'art pour l'art* of acting. The act itself is not of paramount importance here; I mean, it's there, you choose to act in a certain way and must do it well, but the action isn't merely a way of reaching the tangible results in question. The idea is, as Michel Random said, to *act not on the thing but on the soul of the thing*. This idea was divulged in *Japan—Strategy of the Unseen* (1987).

Act not on the thing: the esotericist I envision acts in order to evolve spiritually and mentally, not just for purposes of "staying alive" or even leisure and recreation. Such an actor is never on holiday, never on leave. He lives constantly conscious, constantly relaxed, constantly on the go. Should he need to rest he does so within the framework of the act. As intimated, he knows how to attain peace in action.

Slave on the Triumphal Chariot

A conscious esotericist always has the concept of *Memento Mori* alive in him. "Memento Mori" is Latin and means,

> Remember that you're a mortal. Remember that you're going to die.

According to legend this is what a Roman military commander would hear whispered in his ear when riding his triumphal chariot in the victory parade. When the commander was met by cheers from all and sundry he had a slave standing behind him on the chariot whispering *Memento Mori* in his ear. Otherwise the commander might get hubris, starting to believe that he was more than human, a god.

Counteracting hubris: you have to be aware of your mortality. This brings sobriety to your whole thought, your whole mindset, your whole way of being. Any man needs to have this integrated in his being. And don't get me wrong, it's not about indulging in symbols and moods of death and decay per se. It's about soberly knowing that your physical body one day will cease to function, i.e., "die". The soul lives on but the physical body dies and decays sooner or later. An esotericist has to know this.

I'm not the first one saying this in a philosophical framework. The Existential School of Thought (Sartre, Simone Weil, Heidegger) all had a knowledge of death, of your mortality as a cornerstone of their thought. So if even a nihilist like Sartre acknowledged death then I can't see why this would be so hard to realize for a conscious esotericist.

I'd say: if you've conquered the fear of death then there's no turning back, then you're living the *authentic life* as Heidegger said. And this Castaneda quote puts the matter to a head:

> In a world where death is the hunter, my friend, there is no time for regrets or doubts. There is only time for decisions.[35]

Napoleon

Action is an inner experience. I've already intimated this in this chapter, in the "act not on the thing but on the soul of the thing" meme. Further, you can act in order to get wiser, having the action as a mental elevator. Action can widen your mental concept of a situation, it can bring forth ideas and interpretations you didn't have before the action. This is an aspect of "Action As an Inner Experience" that I cherish. Let's call it the *Napoleonic Modus Operandi*.

Napoleon Bonaparte (1769-1821) was a military commander. The urge of getting going in order to see clearly, of getting a better

---

[35] Castaneda, 1972, p 56.

grasp of a situation, is captured in his motto, *"on s'engage et puis on verra"* ("you engage and then you have a look around"). This meant: in an operational situation, with a pitched battle looming, having made all the basic preparations (like having a logistic base, grasping the layout of the terrain and scouting the whereabouts of the enemy), at some point you also have to get going tactically, you have to approach and tangibly engage the enemy; only thus would the big picture come into view.

This approach to action could be called NAMO—the *Napoleonic Modus Operandi*, the Napoleonic way of operating,

Get Going

The NAMO approach is seen in other contexts than in combat. For instance, in aircraft construction. Having developed a new prototype there comes a time when lab tests, wind-tunnel tests etc. have run their course and someone has to take the prototype for a first flight. It's a highly risky move but it has to be done for any type of aircraft. With all the scientific plans, the concept of how the vessel will perform, the optimal layout of the system having been perfected on the ground, there comes a time when a test pilot "has to take the lady for a spin" and see how it performs in relation to all three dimensions, and in relation to gravity and wind. The plane has to be flown.

We also see this in novel writing. The SF author E. E. Smith (1890-1965) sometimes wrote a synopsis before writing his novels but he soon found that this was redundant, it was impossible to outline all the plot moves and emotional flows of the story. In the 1930s Smith once wrote a detailed synopsis to a series of novels (The Lensman Series), an outline with "peaks of emotional intensity and the valleys of characterization and background material."[36] He himself noted, however, that he was never able to follow any of his outlines at all closely, as the "characters get away from me and do

---

[36] Smith, 1947, p 86.

exactly as they damn please."[37] This to me is an illustration of the relevance of the "Napoleonic Modus Operandi," of not focusing on too detailed preparations but rather having to get going with the project proper, all in order to have the whole being structured as you go.

Jünger

A man steeped in the concept of action as an inner phenomenon is Ernst Jünger (1895-1998). In 1922 he wrote *Der Kampf als inneres Erlebnis* (*Battle As an Inner Experience*). He had the same inspirational, holistic attitude to combat intimated above. Once engaged in combat the soldier is elevated to a higher plane, he is in a sort of glorified trance. As I wrote in my Jünger biography:

> For the elite soldier combat becomes a spiritual act, something of a super meditation. You live on the edge, in the process raising yourself mentally.[38]

I also wrote this on the mindset of a soldier, giving us a clue on the holistic way of acting:

> So what is the mindset of a soldier? It's having the willpower to endure. It's about looking inside, searching inside yourself for those inner reserves that make you go on even if you're hungry, tired and scared. Fighting horror means coping with the reality of death. That's what every soldier has to learn or else he won't last long in the combat zone. It's about getting used to the idea of dying, knowing you're in the Valley of the Shadow of Death. Then what, what about the intimated raising of the spirit, this spiritual experience per se when you fight? Jünger compares it to intoxication and ecstasy, like the ones experienced by poets and saints and even loving couples.[39]

---

[37] Ibid.

[38] Svensson, 2014, p 84.

[39] Ibid.

I'm examining the phenomenon of having to get going in order to function optimally, of not relying too much on minute preparations. The same trait is indicated in the saying of the military commander Helmuth von Moltke (1848-1916). He meant: "No plan survives the first fifteen minutes of contact with the enemy." No plan is fail-safe, the effects of action are unpredictable. So you have to get going in order to grasp the big picture, educating yourself as you go.

NAMO

That was some notes on the Napoleonic Modus Operandi. For its part, an "anti-Napoleonic" modus operandi would be to have a plan of operation delineating how to act in response to every conceivable move and counter-move of the enemy, which is impossible to foresee.

The Napoleonic Modus Operandi is about this: to get going in order to gain a clearer view of it all. Then, having gotten this clearer view, what to do?

You (1) choose to go on or (2) you pull out, declining not to do battle. And in order to reach decision (1) you have to have a premonition of victory. You have to have a concept of winning before earnestly beginning your operation. Don't go ahead blindly.

Winning: you have to know how to win. Conversely, if you have an inkling that a certain operation will fail, then don't perform it. An esotericist of my ilk is no "action at every cost, attack, always attack" operator. Victory is his goal and if he doesn't see it ahead, then he shouldn't even enter a certain arena. A Castaneda quote comes in handy here: "Sorcerers have only one path open to them: to succeed in whatever they do."[40] This includes having the responsibility to decline performing a certain act. You always act, always choose; a smooth operator chooses his battles.

---

[40] *The Sorcerer's Crossing*, p 207.

Castaneda

In the books of Carlos Castaneda there are several quotes in sync with the operational lifestyle. The just quoted *The Sorcerer's Crossing* is written by Taisha Abelar, a woman becoming part of the magic circle led by Don Juan Matus. In Abelar's book the Don Juan figure is called John Michael Abelar. In the same cirle is one Dilas Grau, and this is the man who in his own books calls himself Carlos Castaneda (1925-1998).

In his apprenticeship to become a shaman, a "Nagual", a "Man of Knowledge," Castaneda noted the sayings of his teacher Don Juan, the notes often becoming a doctrine of raising yourself mentally. A mental elevation can be reached by acting in trance, gaining knowledge by performing intelligence operations. For instance, a Man of Knowledge has to be a Warrior, that is, have an operational approach to life. The Man of Knowledge is a kind of "operational esotericist". No complaining, just do it, that's the way, Don Juan says:

> Only as a warrior can one withstand the path of knowledge. A warrior cannot complain or regret anything. His life is an endless challenge, and challenges cannot possibly be good or bad. Challenges are simply challenges.[41]

If you act with zest and pizazz you may reach the glorified trance of heightened awareness, realizing that in this state, living on the edge, everything becomes clearer. Don Juan says to Castaneda:

> I would say that the best of us always comes out when we are against the wall, when we feel the sword dangling overhead. Personally, I wouldn't have it any other way.[42]

---

[41] Castaneda, 1974, p 108.

[42] Ibid p 146.

Warrior Mindset

As I said in the Introduction, if the reader is a Chaos Person, a nihilist materialist with Chaos inside, then there's the risk of my creed being misinterpreted. But if the reader is or aspires to become an Aristocrat of the Soul, a man with Order inside, then there's no risk. Therefore I sometimes use military similes when I teach my creed. Like Castaneda by way of Don Juan saying that the Man of Knowledge shall think, act and be like a warrior. He has to have a warrior mindset. And this is summed up fine in this quote from *The Teachings of Don Juan – A Yaqui Way of Knowledge*:

> A man goes to knowledge as he goes to war, wide awake, with fear, with respect, and with absolute assurance. Going to knowledge or going to war in any other manner is a mistake, and whoever makes it might never live to regret it.[43]

The warrior mindset has its points. For instance, we often talk about "the moral equivalent of war," engendering a state of mind that raises the individual to perform beyond his limitations, and this is why "to be a warrior" is a useful metaphor. And the just quoted Castaneda lines capture this: to "mentally stand on your toes," to shape up before the task, to voluntarily increase your mental energy before the tasks of exploring the spiritual universe.

Finally two quotes mirroring the active approach in Castaneda's books. Above I quoted some lines about challenges and here are more of the same, from *Tales of Power*, one of the best book in the series:

> The basic difference between an ordinary man and a warrior is that a warrior takes everything as a challenge while an ordinary man takes everything as a blessing or a curse.[44]

---

[43] Castaneda, 1968, p 52.

[44] Castaneda, 1974, p 109.

To act raises you mentally. You have to get going, you can't always sit around your friends babbling: "[A] man of knowledge lives by acting, not by thinking about acting."[45]

RAWALTAFA

The esotericist life I envision is the opposite of being a passive nihilist and a mindless materialist. More on the materialist, chaotic mindset in the next chapter. But I don't condemn people having gone astray on the mindless path. It's human to err. As individuals I forgive people sporting a defeatist attitude. Also, it's better to act wrongly and learn from the experience than not acting at all.

I say it again: *it's better to act wrongly and learn from it than not acting at all*. This wisdom can be made into a motto: "Rather Acting Wrongly And Learning Than Abstaining From Action," with RAWALTAFA as an acronym. As you can see the action element is here, stressing the need to get out and get going, "tearing your nails bloody on the wall of existence" as Edith Södergran said. With this she meant that you have to live your life as a trial and error exercise.

It's said that "we come here to learn". In the *samsâra* of existence we live life after life, all the time getting better at it in the school of karma. Conversely, the worst conduct is to only live theoretically, trying to reach moral perfection merely by studying discourses on ethics, "dreaming of systems so perfect that no one will need to be good".[46]

---

[45] 1971, p 90.

[46] T. S. Eliot, "Choruses from The Rock", 1934.

17. THE CHAOTIC MINDSET

In this book I've delineated ideals of ontology and ethics. You could say that I've based my ethics in ontology, having a vision of the Divine Light mirrored in individuals acknowledging this Light within themselves. Conversely, how would an ethic not acknowledging this Light look like? Answer: it would be a disharmonious moral, labeled as the Chaotic Mindset.

The subject of this chapter is The Chaotic Mindset. I'm against this. I criticize this attitude and use it as a counterpart to my ideal in life. And in doing this, sketching the Chaotic Mindset, the goal is to pinpoint the mindset per se, not the persons living it. So in order to be crystal clear as for my general attitude toward my fellow men, I say: I'm not condemning the chaotic person as an individual, as a private person. I'm only opposing the approach in question, the attitude to be labeled as *chaotic, passively nihilist, materialist*.

Zeitgeist

The Chaotic Mindset is the antithesis of the Esoteric Mindset. Esotericism is essentially based in order, beauty and harmony.

Therefore, its counterpart is chaos, disorder and—ultimately—ugliness.

Today the Zeitgeist is in the throes of this chaos and confusion. A new sense of order is needed, a responsibility for the things in life that promote structure and harmony. In short, we need a more spiritual, holistic outlook. So, in order to know the ills of our times, let's take a look at the opposite of Esotericism which is *The Chaotic Mindset*.

A person applying the Chaotic Mindset is negative, nihilistic, ironic, materialistic, atheistic and spiritually passive, having a penchant for apathy. A man with a Chaotic Mindset is an actor having chaos inside him and projecting it to the outer world, affecting people to become passive nihilists and defeatists too. The Chaotic Mindset can engender the roles of a warmonger ("a major war will break out and we're all going to die"), a pessimist ("there's no use in trying, it has been done before, all that exists is the death of the body and the decay of matter") and a reductionist, denying the validity of the holistic paradigm, spiritualism and esotericism ("materialist science has brought us tangible affluence and welfare, spiritualism for its part is about chimeras"). The Chaotic Mindset, prevalent in a materialist denying the Inner Realm, prevents the understanding of the concept of God being within, of the individual soul being part of the All-soul. A man with a Chaotic Mindset conceives God as an external force—and since he can't discern God in the outer world, then he thinks he has disproved the existence of God for all time.

Reservations

Here some reservations are needed. For instance, not all forms of nihilism are bad. Ernst Jünger (in *Über die Linie*, 1950) said that nihilism can be a useful transit zone from a school book idealist having been disillusioned by "this world of sham, debauchery, crime and treason" to a more active existentialist, finding order and light within himself. Julius Evola also had a keen eye for nihilism.

In *Ride the Tiger* (1961) he interpreted the philosophy of Nietzsche's *Thus Spake Zarathustra* and *The Will to Power* as an active nihilism, the mindset of a man having seen through the dogmas of official religion and instead relying on himself, on his own creating "meaning in a meaningless world".

So I'm not against all varieties of nihilism. Even atheism might have a spiritual value. French philosopher Simone Weil (1909-1943), an esoterically gifted existentialist, posited the idea of "atheism as purification".[47] In order not to fall down in complacency as a god believer, in order to avoid a smug, self-satisfied spirituality, bent on feeling the union with God and being content with that, the esotericist could use the concept of atheism—the idea of there being no God, no spiritual, eternal foundation for reality, of there being no Primeval Light of which your soul is a spark—as a means of mentally sobering up.

The "atheism as purification" as an exercise might be done by thinking thus: "What if there were no God, no Primeval Light, no Eternal Forms—how would I think and act right now?"

So I'd say: this way of spiritually seeing things contrariwise, vice versa and the other way around could be a strengthening and edifying modus operandi for a traditional esotericist, for a practitioner of *Prisca Theologia*, a follower of the Eternal Doctrine. The divinely led person explores, develops and fosters his union with God in practicing "atheism as purification" in this way.

Also, to act morally wrong is no transgression, no taboo. It's better to act wrongly and learn from the experience than not acting at all. I've already elaborated on this the previous chapter. I called the concept RAWALTAFA: "Rather Acting Wrongly And Learning Than Abstaining From Action".

No War

The Chaotic Mindset. We find this all around us these days. The chaotically minded scare us with Major War, which in itself is

---

[47] In *La pesanteur et la grâce*, 1947.

absurd since a major war can't erupt after 11/11 2011, which was the beginning of Sat Yuga, the era of peace, truth and compassion starting on this day, following the Kâli Yuga of war, hate and materialism that preceded it. Chaos People typically occupy the positions of Mainstream Media (MSM), constantly scaring us with comets, plagues (remember Ebola?) and the possibility of the sun going nova. The last thing is in itself an impossibility because our sun is to small to go nova. But the Chaos People don't know that, they live in darkness and confusion, and so they spread their word to their brothers in spirit who take up on their memes and spread them further on blogs, forums and social media.

Chaos People are materialist nihilists, happy in their atheistic despair. Again, I don't condemn individuals who are caught in this quagmire of darkness and despondency. I condemn the role and function of the Chaotic Mindset. And in order to end this chapter on a happy note, hereby some tips in avoiding these people and their actions.

The first thing, for example, is stop reading MSM. The Westworld is to a very large extent in the claws of MSM and this results in mental illness, a sense of general unhappiness and angst among the population. Contrariwise, in India and China people are less affected and steered by MSM and subsequently the mental quality of life in those countries are higher than in the West-world.

A more subtle way of countering the influence of the Chaotic Mindset is *rhythm*. The Japanese swordsman Miyamoto Musashi said that in a duel you always move to a rhythm, your own or that of your opponent. So if you're an internet surfer who tends to get hooked to the atmosphere of negative, pessimistic, defeatist sites, ask yourself: "Now that I'm on this site, am I doing what I really want, am I thriving as a person or am I feeling miserable; am I moving to my own rhythm or am I in the throes of someone else's rhythm?"

This is the core issue of being an independent person, of existing in reality. Ask yourself: are you the person you want to be? The answer in this case might be: if you continue to read pessimistic gibberish on MSM sites you might become the victim of the Chaotic Mindset. But if you choose to leave such sites and start reading constructive material instead, you begin to move in your own rhythm, in the process being on the way of becoming an Authentic Person, maybe even an Aristocrat of the Soul.

As for reading constructive material it doesn't have to be expressly uplifting, programmatic material like the Bhagavad-Gîtâ, The Gospels, The Edda or whatever. It might just be neutral info about things you're interested in. The internet has a lot of fairly neutral, fact-oriented sites suitable for pleasure reading, like encyclopaedias.

Avoiding Chaos

If you have persons sporting a Chaotic Mindset in your own social environment, avoid them. People draining you of energy must be avoided. People dragging you down into a miasma of pessimism, defeatism and despair must either be helped out of their despondency or avoided altogether. We should of course be ready to help our neighbor. Love thy neighbor, as the Scripture says. But in full it says: Love thy neighbor *as yourself*. You have to be able to thrive as an individual before you can help others. I elaborated on this in chapter fourteen when I discussed compassion. Also, some people are born pessimists, like some are born optimists.

In Canto XIII Ezra Pound wrote: "If a man have not order within him / he can not spread order about him." I touched upon this phenomenon in the beginning of this chapter. Now you have the idea more elegantly worded. And style aside, this is the gist of living the reflected life, the esotericist life: you have to have order within, living the volitional life in order to gain control over your thoughts, desires and emotions. On the contrary, to just let go and follow your impulses, merely living on hope and drifting here and there with the tide of the times, this will drain you of energy and have you end up in The Chaos Company.

Sentimental Materialism

Materialism ultimately tends to chaos. No kind of order and structure can arise from matter itself. In order to install order and harmony there has to be an influence from higher, more advanced, more energetically subtle levels.

This I've intimated in chapters 5-9, when I treated modern physics. Materialism is an idea leading to confusion and darkness. And yet, many materialistic persons are affable persons in themselves, they have families that they care for, they can pursue careers and create things of use to other people. How, then, do we explain this? One way of seeing it is to label these persons as "sentimental materialists". This was done by Rudolf Steiner once. And this is clarifying. You could say: people aren't *logical*, they're *sociological*. Some materialists want to keep some traditional, esoterically based ideas of order and harmony, but they lack the ability to wholly subsume themselves into this, refusing to see themselves as *Seiendes im Sein,* as soul sparks of the Primeval Light.

They refuse to see the Inner Light, "das Vünklein der Seele" that Meister Eckart spoke about. Instead they have "the death of the body and the decay of matter" as fundamentals of existence. "When we die everything goes black" is the creed. But still, they have feelings for art and beauty, for fellow human beings, for tradition and history. They are sentimental within a materialist *Weltanschauung*. Again, I don't condemn individuals holding this view but I do condemn sentimental materialism per se as an aberration. Instead, I'd say, be consistent, acknowledge the esoteric source of beauty, truth and compassion, recognize the immaterial patterns and structures of the world as being based in a Causal Sphere of higher ontological dignity. Conversely, to see all these examples of order as having appeared spontaneously from matter itself is absurd.

So I'd say: spontaneously nothing good comes out of this world—but spontaneously something good comes *to* this world.

18. CARL JUNG: INTEGRATING THE OPPOSITES

I T'S TRUE THAT Carl Jung (1875-1961) primarily was active as a psychiatrist. You can apply his ideas and theories within a strict psychological framework. There are Jungian analysts professionally active as psychotherapists. And Jungian psychology is a recognized discipline in the Academy. However, Jung was also something of a mystic. This became evident in his memoirs, published in 1961. And since I'm open to esotericism I acknowledge the mystical side of Jung. I endorse many seemingly wayward ideas if they lead to clarity. Jung's general approach to life, art and philosophy is a strong contribution to the Borderline creed.

Jung integrated many apparently conflicting aspects in his system. His thought seems to occupy a gray area between religion, spirituality, psychology and art. There is sometimes the risk of him reducing everything into psychic phenomena but otherwise I deem his *opus* as quite inspiring. I'm no Jungian but Jung can be a refreshing read for the esoterically minded, contemporary traditionalist. Jung was a kind of Gnostic mystic but he made the effort of expressing himself in a way related to the modern reader, not just to the unworldly recluse.

Individuation

A central concept in Jungian psychology is *individuation*. This is a holistic concept. In specifically Jungian terms, it's about *realizing the archetype of wholeness*. It's about becoming a whole, harmonic being. It's about uniting with God.

Of course, to the random esotericist this sounds good. Let's be whole, let's unite with God. But to reach this sublime state you have to walk a long road, it would seem. It's not done by simply kneeling, saying a prayer and be saved. Individuation is a *process*. Wikipedia says that individuation is "the psychological process of integrating the opposites, including the conscious with the unconscious, while still maintaining their relative autonomy."

Further, individuation is about uniting the individual unconscious with the collective unconscious. All this sounds like an integrative approach in sync with the *Borderline* project. But at this stage, you might also have to ask yourself if you really want to take such a ride, delving into the individuation process. What's it really like to dive into the depths of your unconscious with all its fears, nightmares and demons? What's it like to live in humanity's unconscious and meet all the horrors of history and myth? It's all there and in the Jungian way of knowledge there's the need to encounter them and acknowledge them. Discernment is required when wishing to integrate all the opposites of the Inner Mind.

In the Jungian Way of Knowledge you have to admit that you yourself have less attractive traits. This is symbolized by the Shadow, a figure representing suppressed and taboo-related sides of your being. It's having to admit that you're "less than perfect," that you too can have less appealing traits to your character. The trick here is to acknowledge this and move on to your goal, not indulging in darkness per se but realizing that *la condition humaine* is complex. It's not simply about "being good, avoiding bad". Ideals we must have but the Jungian attitude of integrating opposites is a step on the way of knowing ourselves more profoundly.

Gnôthi seauvtón, know thyself; this was the inscription on the Apollo temple in Olympia. Jung's system is rooted in old wisdom like this but expressed in a modern idiom. For instance, as a scientist he didn't expressly speak about "God" but about "the god image in the human mind". That's instructive for being able, as an academic, to discuss unproved concepts like God without being labeled as irrelevant. For as writer Alan Moore (1953-) once wrote, "The one place gods inarguably exist is in the human mind." He had one of his comic book characters say that. After writing this Moore realized that myth and magic are viable occupations and thus he started practicing magic himself. I personally am not into magic, my Way of Knowledge is the artistic-essayist way. But the spiritual mindset of a white magician is closer to me than that of, say, a nihilist materialist.

Mandala

A prime example of Jung employing traditional concepts in his thought is *the mandala*. A mandala is a circle, a central image in far eastern philosophy. The East always has had a penchant for harmony, wholeness and stillness. This is symbolized in mandalas which can depict the world, a learning system, a man—everything. It's the microcosm as a mirror of the macrocosm, it's the whole conceived at every level. Jung for his part acknowledged this eastern attitude of wholeness, stillness and completeness, and in his therapy he encouraged his patients to draw mandalas. He even drew them himself; there are a lot of examples of them in his work. One such that I saw had successive, multicolored circles in the middle and, at the cardinal points, a winged pyramid symbol, a crescent, the cross and the yin-yang symbol. In the spaces in between there were the symbols of Venus, Mars, Jupiter and Saturn.

The meaning of this mandala can be interpreted in various ways. But when both the cross and the yin-yang symbol is there, it means: integrate Western and Eastern spirituality. In your personal thought (and in the culture at large), unify the Eastern way of tranquility and self-centeredness with the Western penchant for freedom and independence. Again, this might seem easy but in reality it's hard. Western philosophy, based in Heraclitus, Plato, Plotinus etc. is written in Greek. So first, learn Greek. Then, learn the western ontological key concepts. Then learn Sanskrit and the totally different metaphysical concepts applied in the East. Then integrate the two. Easy, isn't it...? However, it *can* be done, I can personally vouch for that. And in that process, the image of the mandala adorned with both a cross and a taoist symbol, and some other balancing symbols, might be of help.

To integrate opposites is easy in theory, hard in practice, but it can be done and Carl Jung has shown us the way. And in the mandala he has given us a symbol of the True Self as a microcosm. The mandala is the road to the center, to the individuation, to spiritual fulfillment. "You can't get any further than to the center," Jung meant. This reminds me of a line by Swedish poet Hjalmar Gullberg: "Life is a dream we chase / in a Homeric Homecoming to ourselves."

Mystic

Jung was a holistically minded mystic. His way of knowledge was both complex and simple, both intellectual and artistic. Also, his creed acquired some sectarian traits (q.v. Noll, *The Jung Cult*, 1997) and this might be questionable. I don't support sectarianism and the cult of a guru. But overall Jung's creed was a way to God and as such it was *not* simplistic. There were no ten commandments, no "noble eightfold path" to follow. "Jungianism" is a glorious intellectual challenge. Like in the way it stresses the "integration of the opposites". As intimated this sounds easy but isn't done in a trice.

For example, besides the East-West integration we might have the prospect of "integrating the male with the female". This can be symbolized, as was done above, in surrounding the mandala with the Mars and the Venus sign. Mars is the male force, Venus the female, and both man and woman might benefit from incorporating the opposite in his/her being. In Jungian terms it's done by encountering the *anima*. In his subconscious ventures—in dreams, in art etc.—a man meets his image of the female (*anima*) and a woman meets her image of the male (*animus*). The anima, if we focus on her, in turn can appear as embodiments of different *archetypes* (the young woman, the mother, the wise old woman). Conceptually this is both an example of the archaic roots of Jung's thought (anima, animus and the idea of the archetype have some footing in ancient, Gnostic thought) and of the artistic connections that this can engender. For example, a man reading about a female character in a novel and seeing a movie with a female star relates to his *anima*. In this way Jung has carved out a unique niche in Perennial Thought.

The archetypes, for their part, were of different kinds. First there are archetypal *figures* (such as the eternal youngster, the wise old man, the great mother, the trickster, God). Then there are archetypal *events* (birth, death, separation from the parents, initiation, marriage, the union of opposites). Also, there are archetypal *objects* (snake, water, tree, sun, moon, fire). Finally there can be said to exist archetypal *motifs*, such as the animus, the anima, the shadow and, more generally, the apocalypse, the deluge, the creation.

This is like a store house of plot elements, a possible inventory for things you need to write a novel. And indeed Jungian attitudes are fruitful for creating literary works of art.

God

Jung's system can be seen as a way to God. As an academic researcher he may have used expressions like, "the god image in the human mind" rather than God, period (see above). But the mystic that meets us in his memoirs (*Memories, Dreams, Reflections*) speaks in no uncertain terms about God. For instance, he quotes the Latin saying, "*Vocatus atque non vocatus, Deus aderit*" ("called or not called, God will be there"). This is a fine expression of the omnipresence of God.

Jung was indeed no common god-believer. His memoirs devote several pages to his struggle with the common, parochial God image of his childhood and youth. But in time he learned of the God of the mystics, a more complex, variegated entity of integrated opposites, of male and female, will and thought, action and being. A God with whom we are co-creators of the universe, a God of whom we all carry a light fragment in our souls. We only have to acknowledge this in order for this wonder to be established, confirmed and spread, in an ever ongoing two-way flow.

Recent Reception

In the 1990s Carl Gustaf Jung (1875-1961) was quite *en vogue* in my home country, Sweden. True, the same was the case throughout the Western world, but here I'll concentrate on the Swedish reception. Books by and about Jung were published rather liberally by Swedish imprints. Since then this wave may seem to have abated. But on the whole I think Jung is established in Sweden now. There are Jungian psychoanalysts and Jungian attitudes are allowed within the humanities. Thus, for the contemporary art, religion or psychology student who wants to link his research to traditional attitudes Jungianism might be a way, you could say a fairly established way. Today's academy may be rather nihilistic, reductionist and anti-traditional but Jungianism still offers a tried way to build countermeasures against this.

With Jung at his side any budding academician can become a traditionalist standard-bearer. Jung, I figure, can be seen as a kind of traditionalist. He didn't use the term as Julius Evola and René Guénon did but clearly he was an archaically inclined person such as these gentlemen and others, like Ernst Jünger, Mircea Eliade and D. T. Suzuki, whom he all worked with. The focus in Jung's research was on traditional religions, old documents and eternal issues; then, with his special terminology, he could apply the wisdom of modern psychology, myth research and literature study. This terminology and the Jungian analytical apparatus are fairly viable means for linking today's academy with subjects such as Mazdaism, Gnosticism and Hermeticism as well as more familiar greats like Shakespeare, Wagner, Nietzsche and whatever you as a traditionalist want. The Jungian approach has its proper role for scholars who want to go beyond gender theory, HBTQ issues and the Frankfurt School of thought, the idols of today's Academy.

As I said, in Swedish there were many Jung studies and overviews published in the 1990s. As for the English language Vivianne Crowley's monograph *Principles of Jungian Spirituality* (1998) can symbolize this fairly recent interest in Jung. This is a popular introduction but there has also been translations of Jung's original work such as *Aion, Symbols of Transformation* and *Psychological Types*. But these English translations were made already in the 1970s so I'd say that, in the English speaking world, interest in Carl Jung has been fairly constant since he died in 1961.

Literature

Jung's contribution to human science is large. Here I intend to focus on how to use Jungian method in the study modern fantasy literature, by this exposing some traits that are psychologically and esoterically interesting.

In this respect I particularly think about the existence of *the Shadow* and how it is integrated into one's own being. Jung sketched this image of man's inner life thus: humans have a collective unconscious where there exists eternal patterns or syndromes, known as *archetypes*. The man who wants to deal with the realities of existence must recognize these archetypes, even less pleasant ones such as the Shadow. The Shadow is a figure of the same sex as the person himself (unlike the *Animus* which is always of the opposite sex), a dark, possibly frightening figure who represents repressed and undesirable qualities in oneself. The Shadow is really complex, being able to manifest itself in a thousand different ways. But as a person you should recognize it and in the long run it should be incorporated with the essence of your being. You shouldn't capitulate to it, not altogether becoming it, but you have to affirm its existence. Otherwise you can't become a complete person.

As an acquaintance said: "If you shut out the demons, they will only enter through the back door." Instead, integrating the Shadow is a step on the way to self-realization. Having reached such a wholeness of your being you've completed a concept I've already discussed: *individuation*. To repeat, individuation is the integration of opposites with the individual as a battlefield. Kurt Almqvist (*Att läsa Jung*, 1997) says that individuation doesn't mean moral perfection: it should rather be seen as a quest for integration into a larger whole.

That seems fair. However, I believe that once the Shadow is recognized in this way, you must have the ambition to go ahead and develop further—to perfection. Jung for his part also used alchemy as a metaphor for the mental processes, and there the goal has to be in terms of going from lead to gold, from impure and imperfect to purity and perfection. Here I figure: perfection shouldn't be held forth too early for the striving adept, then he might become frustrated. This might lead to a dualistic lock-up of the type, "Jesus was perfect, I'm only a struggling sinner, I can never reach that level; now I'll become an atheist instead."

So perfection should be recognized, in some or other fashion as a long-term goal. But in this context and on the way to perfection even the Shadow should be recognized. And there's a good example of this in modern fantasy literature. I here think of Ursula Le Guin's *The Wizard of Earthsea* (1968). Le Guin herself may or may not have known about Jung's ideas about The Shadow, but this is unimportant here. Her story is elegantly designed and executed. It doesn't have "the smell of the lamp," as you might otherwise fear will be the result when people are studying Jung and put together stories with well-ordered archetypes in a synchronized plot.

Fantasy

In Le Guin's story the wizard Ged lives in a fairy tale world called *Earthsea*; it's a multitude of scattered islands, therefore the name.

Magic is taught in a particular school and Ged attends its courses to become a white magic operator for the benefit of society, fighting trolls and dragons and other hell-spawn. During his training he happens to conjure a Dark Entity by mistake, a companion he can't shake off. However, after many ifs and buts he confronts this entity, this Shadow. And he does it in the only way that remains when all the other ways are rejected: Ged figures out the shape's real name to be none other than Ged, and by calling this name the figure virtually merges with him.

Whether intentionally Jungian or not this was original as fantasy: it was not just about going out and fighting evil, jousting with and conquering the dragon, and then go home and live as a hero forever. But this, one might think, is what Tolkien for his part is guilty of in his trilogy (*Lord of the Rings*, 1954-56). This is a classic, no doubt about it, but from a human perspective there's something missing here. True, evil has to be combated, but on the human level you have to admit that anyone, including the hero, can be tempted by evil. The darkness in Tolkien's tale pursues a somewhat secluded, monolithic existence as Far Away Horrors. Now, I don't demand that the trilogy should have included a scene where Frodo meets Sauron and the latter says, "Frodo, I am your father." But some form of extra, psychological depth could have been needed in this respect.

Of course Tolkien did have some depth. For instance, the conflict Gandalf-Saruman have hints of this confrontation with the Shadow. But the central narrative with Frodo as ring bearer-cum-destroyer lacks the meeting with the Shadow. The end at Mount Doom is mythologically poignant, it gets kind of elementary and mythic in itself and that's fine. But you could also have imagined and end with strains of psychology, sporting a confrontation with the Sauron figure, this perhaps lacking in the symbolic quality of destroying the ring in the fire that forged it, but on the whole giving it more existential depth.

Integrating the Shadow

As for Tolkien's text you can say: Frodo has fought and defeated evil on such an elementary plane that he can't remain in Middle-Earth afterwards. He has done a deed worthy of a demigod. And so he goes to the Immortal Countries of the West at the end. It's the logical path to take for an incarnation of goodness, for an agent elevated above everyday life. A more human hero would however need some form of integration of his Jungian shadow to seem credible. As Ged in Le Guin's story. Or a certain Graf Ulrich von Bek in Michael Moorcock's *The War Hound and the World's Pain* (1982). There the hero meets Lucifer in the beginning, a creature claiming to be misunderstood by God. von Bek is given by Lucifer the mission to retrieve the Grail to offer to God as a conciliatory gesture.

This strikes me as rather original. It's like *Faust* in concise fantasy form. It shows how the hero may have to face the darkness in order to develop and reach, not moral perfection, but some kind of wholeness. Moorcock's novel celebrates some spiritual triumphs in this respect, although the author personally states that he's an agnostic intellectual.

Moorcock's novel shows us that even the hero can have darkness within himself. This, to me, is the individual as battlefield for the fight between good and evil. This is what the Shadow and its integration is about.

Campbell

Above I hinted the movie line, "I am your father". As everyone knows it's the villain Darth Vader who says it to Luke Skywalker in the film *Return of the Jedi* (1983).

This is big league integration of the Shadow, I daresay...! The creator of Star Wars, George Lucas, certainly had a Jungian strain in his work. For in the early 70s he wrote a first draft of the script and then he looked up Joseph Campbell's myth study *The Hero*

With a Thousand Faces (1949). Campbell was a Jungian influenced American scholar. And with reference to Campbell Lucas saw that his own story had some timeless depths. Campbell's Jungian construed hero archetype is one that was suggested above: one that goes off to fight the monster but also learns something about himself in the process. The hero then can return to his everyday life as a more complete person, possibly as "a sadder and a wiser man" (Coleridge). Or possibly as an integrated personality, one who has undergone Jungian individuation.

To sound out the depths of an artwork with Jung's help is a big topic. I will therefore end this chapter here and simply suggest some further reading, concentrating on one book: Jung's memoir, *Memoirs, Dreams, Reflections* (1962, German original the previous year). This is exemplary in every respect. Dreams play a central role in them. Imagine a combination of the dream descriptions Ernst Jünger offers in his diaries and Swedenborg's *Dream Journal*, all within the context of a psychological research zeal and with a bit of Gnosticism, Hermeticism and alchemy added, and you have Jung's memoirs in a nutshell. The book is highly recommended for each reader with an interest in psychology, myth and religion. It's a good read with spiritual depth, almost something of a western, scholarly Carlos Castaneda.

19. NIETZSCHE: NO ORDINARY ATHEIST

GERMAN PHILOSOPHER Friedrich Nietzsche (1844-1900) can't be bypassed in a Borderline study like this. His thought can be interpreted both as nihilistic and as spiritual. Modern and conservative minds alike refer to his ideas. Also, Nietzsche existed in the gray area between systematic thought and art. His philosophical novel *Thus Spake Zarathustra* is both an existential tale and a showcase of ethical and moral thought. In this chapter I'll try to encompass some conflicting strains of Nietzsche's thought, showcasing the German as something of an Integral Esotericist.

Safranski

Were there idealistic strains to the philosophy of Friedrich Nietzsche? Indeed there were. Rüdiger Safranski's *Nietzsche - A Philosophical Biography* (2003) presents an image of Nietzsche as existing in the gray area between nihilism and idealism.

Nietzsche went to the core of the matter concerning atheism. He took atheism seriously. But still, Nietzsche the atheist can't do without concepts of the divine. For instance, in *Thus Spoke Zarathustra* (1885) is mentioned elements such as "my soul trembles of divine desires," and "I adore thee, O eternity"; not exactly the usual sayings of an atheist. And on the philosophical plane may be mentioned that despite his biologism Nietzsche speaks out against Darwin. Why? For instance, the Englishman had forgotten the *spirit* that Nietzsche writes of in *Twilight of the Gods* (1889). According to Safranski, Nietzsche accuses Darwin that he has transferred the unconsciously acting development in the animal kingdom to the human kingdom. This, to Nietzsche, drags the human realm down into blindly working processes. Man is conscious and he develops himself consciously, is what Nietzsche means. Man as a thinking being driven by will doesn't depend on natural processes, he's free and can create anything, including his own future being.

Man can overcome himself, Nietzsche means. The concept of "the Superman" can be seen as a man having supreme command of himself. A "responsible man" if you will. A man exerting the Will to Power over himself, like a yoga master, a *sannyasin* or a *swami*. True, there are atheistic yoga masters too, but this Nietzschean way to knowledge is no common atheism.

According to Safranski Nietzsche spoke about affirming one's virtues, affirming the creative force and imagination you have within. The Zarathustra character shines like the sun, he wants to give light and joy to his fellow men. Zarathustra also spoke about transforming yourself from a camel (a student gathering existing wisdom and carrying it like a load) to a lion (a heroic, creative spirit giving his view of things) to, finally, a playing child, having access to the primeval sources of creativity and joy. Again, this is not what you commonly associate with atheism.

Of course there can be virtuous, creative etc. atheists too. And Nietzsche did indeed say that God was dead. But this last saying is absurd, at least to me. God is within, we all have the soul spark, "das Vünklein der Seele". And according to Safranski the Superman isn't free from religion, he hasn't lost it; instead, he has taken it back into himself. The common nihilist on the other hand, "the last man," he has truly lost his religion and remains vegetating in his everyday, devoid of hope, ideals and dreams. "The last man" is a concept presented in *Thus Spake Zarathustra*.

Compassion

"Man, you can not live without compassion." Dostoyevsky said this. But Nietzsche wasn't listening. Safranski argues that Nietzsche had some difficulties in getting rid of this notion, compassion, so central to Christianity. The German's wrestling with it can be seen in *Ecce Homo*. And wasn't it symptomatic that Nietzsche, both the person and his philosophy (which are difficult to distinguish, no other philosopher has used the word "I" as often as he) broke down when he was visited by compassion at the sight of a horse that was whipped by its driver? This was in Turin, Italy; the Superman himself fell weeping on the neck of the animal to protect it—and then it was over with Nietzsche. In the clinical sense he went insane, having to live in nursing homes or being cared for at home the rest of his life.

Away with all compassion, that was Nietzsche's bold philosophy, worship yourself as a creative genius...! And in passing, one can pronounce the death of God; then the stage is open to great deeds... But to dethrone God while at the same time "keeping it real," maintaining a sense of authenticity and pathos that Nietzsche did, then you're in hot water. For, if atheist life shouldn't be flat and dull, guided by necessity and the demands of everyday life, you have to put someone else on the vacant throne—for example, yourself. After his collapse Nietzsche indeed wrote the following to his old friend, Professor Jacob Burckhardt:

> After all, I would much prefer to be a professor in Basel than God; but I haven't dared to push my private religion so far that, in fulfilling it, I would neglect the creation of the world. As you can see, you have to make sacrifices, where ever and however you live. [Letter 6/1 1889]

Nihilism

Nietzsche went to the core of the matter concerning atheism. This I said above. Philosophically, this can be seen as an embracing of nihilism.

Nihilism is the idea that nothing (Latin *nihil*) spiritual exists. The only fundamentals in life are the death of the body and the decay of matter. You get born, you live and then you die; everything becomes dark when you die, no soul lives on, nothing. So how to cope in such a nihilistic world, a world without values, without spiritual goals, without transcendent truths? Unlike other materialists Nietzsche didn't sentimentally adhere to reverse-engineered, secular values like "humanism, brotherly love, justice as fairness". The freedom of the nihilist was essentially shattering. Nietzsche realized that if you've dethroned God and made yourself free then angst and dejection can ambush you and destroy you.

In *Thus Spake Zarathustra* (I.17, "The Way of the Creating One") Nietzsche addresses a man having escaped from slavery. But are you free, is the question, really free? What, in essence, are you free from? Not many of today's freedom-loving individuals can answer that question satisfactorily. And they would cringe if people like me said that freedom is to acknowledge your divine nature, your Inner Light.

You have to *deserve* to be free. Without a conception of *Sein*, of Willpower and how to use it, a "free" man soon becomes a slave again, slave to materialism, slave to his desires.

Atheism

Was Nietzsche the atheist proclaiming himself to be God, the reborn Dionysus? If so, I lift my hat to this boldness, of taking the denial of the current god to its ultimate consequences. Put bluntly, and not denying that there are atheist of the pious, fruitful kind, I'd say: there has only been one atheist and his name was Friedrich Nietzsche.

But for us mere mortals then, what's left of Nietzsche's doctrine when you see his personal destiny? When you see the aspects of hubris, the shrill and insistent tone present even in *Thus Spake Zarathustra*, when you see how Nietzsche overestimated himself? Indeed, you can find negative traits in Nietzsche's late opus. But here we're looking for the positive.

Already mentioned is "the will to power," reinterpreted as "the will to power over yourself": then you leave out all the chauvinist associations and instead end up in asceticism. Reportedly Nietzsche held a secret admiration for this attitude to life.

We have also seen how Nietzsche cherished creativity: get back to the child and his playing, that's the Fountainhead of artistic creation. Zarathustra always spoke of *the dance* as the rhythm of life. He had no respect for thinkers *who couldn't dance*, which is an original aspect of philosophy.

And pronouncing a god as dead is rather meaningless. Nietzsche himself said in a youth-hood poem: "Von grosse dingen zweigt man, oder reder gross" ("of great things you keep silent or speak great."). I rest my case. Also, speaking of gods: Nietzsche adored Dionysus—a god who indeed died but then was resurrected. Also, Nietzsche spoke about things "beyond Good and Evil" in "Jenseits von Gut und Böse" (book title, 1886)—and personally I'd say that this is *my* God, existing beyond everyday good and evil. And didn't Heraclitus, the pre-Socratic thinker Nietzsche held in high esteem, maintain a similar God image...?

Style

Nietzsche wanted to transform philosophy into "a cheerful science" (*Die fröhliche Wissenschaft*, 1882). He showed that it mustn't be banished to the Academies, in them being something of a reactive, negative, dissecting venture, performed by people driven by ressentiment and dissatisfaction. In his day it was the Hegelian legacy he fought, a solidified idealism without room for the individual's free will. Nietzsche, for his part, emphasized the individual, the feeling and the personal experience. He admitted his role as a subject and spurned philistine objectivity. Like before him Kierkegaard and Socrates, he seems to have held that the meaning of philosophy is to philosophize. The answers you might not reach, but the base of it all is and will remain to be an individual who asks the questions, acknowledging his limitations and based on this expands out indefinitely—to selfishness and hubris on the one hand, and to identity and self-hood on the other.

Nietzsche stylized himself, stylized his quest for the benefit of us mortals, we who are left here on this earth and reading his books. He's often funny, sometimes bantering, but no one can err on the style: in all his books it is Nietzsche, from beginning to end: "l'homme et la style c'est la même". The man and the style is the same.

Nietzsche stylized himself into a symbol. He took his personal philosophy and made it into an artwork. The chief example of this is *Thus Spake Zarathustra*, by someone aptly called "philosophical novel".

Dionysus

I just mentioned Dionysus. A recent study highlights Nietzsche's attitude to this Greek god. To me this affirms that Nietzsche was no common reductionist, no simpleton atheist of the current kind.

The study in question is Abir Taha's *Nietzsche's Coming God— Or the Redemption of the Divine* (2013). Here we find the above sketched theme of Nietzsche's view on divinity, of the declaring that God is dead as a positive, creative act. Taha:

> The will to power is essentially a will to self-overcoming, the will to create and recreate—Gods. Therefore God shall be reborn in a new form, in conformity with the Nietzschean (Dionysian) principle of eternal recurrence and eternal creation."[48]

Nietzsche becomes more than a mere critic of religion, he becomes a prophet, as Gwendolyn Taunton shows in her review of Taha's book.[49]

---

[48] Taha, p 83.

[49] Taunton, G., Nietzsche's Coming God in *Aristokratia III*, ed. Deva, K., Manticore Press, 2014, p 312

In Taunton's mind this highlights the very nature of Nietzsche's *Thus Spake Zarathustra,* this book "where Zarathustra clearly occupies a prophetic role" (Taunton). Nietzsche becomes a sort of prophet declaring the return of Dionysus, a life-affirming force in contrast to the perceived feebleness of Christianity. Taha, for her part, concludes that Nietzsche wasn't an atheist à la modern skeptics and pessimists but instead someone pronouncing the prevailing god dead in favor of a spiritual awakening of Dionysus.

Pagan aspects aside, this again would suggest that Nietzsche was no ordinary atheist, no mere denier of the existence of god and / or gods. Instead, he affirmed the reality of such a being as Dionysus. In acknowledging divine traits Nietzsche found freedom and strength of spirit. Conversely, Christianity to him came to represent a slave moral giving rise to nihilism, sterility and banality. Although I personally can't see all this in Christianity Taha's outline gives me the impetus to summarize Nietzsche's spirituality like this.

First, Nietzsche was no run-of-the-mill atheist merely showing us the way into nothingness. Instead he preached an antithesis to all what modern atheism represents—ressentiment, negativity and nihilism—by stressing willpower, artistry and pizazz as necessary elements of a philosophy of life. Secondly, he revitalized a spiritual life solidified and stagnant due to an official religion, Christianity, having focused almost all its effort on ritual, mythology and a watered-down version of the existential teaching of Christ.

Evola on Nietzsche

In the rest of this chapter I'll focus on the Nietzsche critique formulated by Julius Evola (1898-1974). Specifically, in *Ride the Tiger* (1961) Evola had an integrative outlook on Nietzsche's ethics, fitting for the book you're now reading—*Borderline*.

Ideally, the Nietzschean ethics can be described as the modus operandi for an Aristocrat of the Soul. Someone even described Nietzsche's outlook as *aristocratic radicalism*. In *Ride the Tiger,* Evola tried to discern the fruitful trait of this ethics. For instance, the Italian described it as *the energy of Dionysus balanced by the sublimity of Apollo*.

Dionysus and Apollo: these figures Nietzsche himself had employed in his study of the tragedy plays of ancient Greece, *The Birth of Tragedy* (1872). Nietzsche maintained that these plays, primarily the ones by Aischylos, had their specificity in a combination of the expressiveness of Dionysus, the wine-god with his ecstatic followers, and the moderation and elevation of Apollo, the god of light. From this aspect, Evola's ideal view of Nietzschean ethics became "an integrated and rectified Dionysism".[50] As for Nietzsche he spurned idealist philosophy (including *die Seinsphilosophie* I cherish) and based his moral on "life," in living your life instinctively and "being faithful to earth," but according to Evola this might lead to emptiness and desolation. Thus, the orgiastic Dionysianism needs to be tempered and balanced by a reflective spirit, and to have it symbolized by Apollo is a conceptual tour-de-force, making the Nietzschean ethics credible on its own terms.

Tragic Optimism

In Evola's ideological and philosophical coda, *Ride the Tiger*, the outlook is about the dimension of spiritual versus material, the essentials of existence. Any ideology or personal philosophy must begin here. Our materialistic civilization is about to fall. And *Ride the Tiger* in this respect says that the best thing is to accelerate the decay of this Iron Age, this Kâli Yuga. Evola is pessimistic about the development in general but an optimist with regard to individual players, the Aristocrats of the Soul who have order within themselves.

You can say: like Nietzsche Evola is a *tragic optimist*.

Earlier in *Borderline* I've talked about Kâli Yuga and Sat Yuga. Evola too acknowledges these concepts. He says: this *succession of the ages* must take its course. The paradise of the Golden Age,

---
[50] Evola, 1961, p 71.

followed by the progressively less spiritual Silver, Copper and Iron ages, is the pattern of the degeneration of human cultures. One finds this schedule in Hesiod. And in Hindu mythology; in the latter context the last stage is called the Age of Death (the Kâli Yuga). This process of succession must take its course. But those who stand firm in the Kâli Yuga challenges will find themselves well fit to live in the following Golden Age, the truth era of Sat Yuga.

Evola had many pet ideas during his career as an ideologue and philosopher. One of his ideas, still upheld when he wrote *Ride the Tiger*, was about the supremacy of the warrior class over the priest class. Evola, unlike René Guénon who stressed the role of priests, saw the warrior class as spiritually superior. For his part, Guénon's recipe was: doctrine, faith and the supremacy of priests. Evola's was: pragmatism and means to achieve goals, no doctrines are needed...! Evola saw the Guénon attitude as a bowing before empty altars. The traditional, exoteric religions (organized Christianity, Islam, Buddhism, etc.) were supposedly dead forms. Against this Evola stressed esoteric traditions such as alchemy, hermeticism, magic and tantra. But they would be rooted in tradition and not in the form of new age theosophy, nor in the form of a romantic yearning for medieval times or latter-day paganism.

In line with this Evolian outlook the politics of today are meaningless. We live in a political interregnum where politics only administer a dead materialism with "increased growth" as the number one priority. In such a situation the time is right for an aristocrat to improve himself spiritually, to focus on his own person.

The Nihilist Outlook

Ride the Tiger covers the development of modern thought. A centerpiece is held by *nihilism*. In the topic at hand, Nietzsche's ethics, Evola emphasizes that Nietzsche's nihilism was active, not passive. Another right-wing thinker, Ernst Jünger, focused on the same trait in *Über die Linie* (1950).

Jünger also had read Nietzsche. Jünger noted how nihilism in this context can serve as a purification, a phase where you, as a traditionalist, have the time to fathom that the old world is dead, and that in the new world you need new strategies to live a traditionally inspired life. These new strategies have as their base any kind of esotericism, any attitude forcing the individual to seek power, reality and tranquility within.

~

Let's look at the current state of nihilism, with guidance from the outlines of *Ride the Tiger*. You could say: for the average modern man nihilism is no problem. We're born into its world-view: everything is meaningless, enjoy yourself while you can, then you die and nothing lives on; your body dies and matter decays, alleluia. This is nihilism (of Lat. *nihil*, nothing), the idea that there are no eternal values, no transcendental reality and thus no essential point in living a reflected life. And for most people this is no stumbling block. Today, in the Academy and the arts, it's taken off the agenda. The man sporting spiritual values is seen as a man ruled by phantoms, a man not worth taking seriously. The goal for both left and right is to increase economic growth. Materialism reigns supreme.

We are born, we live and we die and that's all there is to it. The meaning of life is to acquire gadgets and enjoy yourself. The contemporaries of Nietzsche, the late 1800s and early 1900s people, could still be shocked and intimidated by such an outlook, by nihilism as an idea: a world without eternal values would mean that there essentially is nothing to live for. This was an unpleasant awakening from the petty-bourgeois world of comfort. At the same time other, more adventurous spirits, could see this smashing of religion and conservatism as steps on the road to true liberation: Now, a new, fairer world could be built, free from the bourgeois world of untruthful facades, and in all fairness this analysis often rang true since much of the bourgeois world was essentially materialistic.

What, then, happened to this secular vision of a "new, fairer world," this mainstream recycling of idealism? According to the Evolian outlook, this reversed-engineered, non-religious "meaningful cosmos" of the, say, inter-war years, was in turn absorbed by a new, expressly materialist attitude in the form of Marxism. And Marxism was hostile to all forms of tradition, spirituality and traditional values of duty, honor and self-restraint. Marxism became *default mode* for the western intelligentsia after the 1968 surge.

Today's "nihilist type 1A" isn't even that idealistic. He considers himself to live in a meaningless world where one at most can create a viable private morality, à la French existentialism where we live in an empty, godless world with individuals "condemned to freedom," as Sartre said.

Evola however affirmed the freedom of this post-bourgeois world. And he did it by stressing the active nihilism of Nietzsche.

Being Free

Essentially, nihilism takes a strong mind to endure. In *Der Wille zur Macht* Nietzsche saw nihilism as a kind of test. A spiritual nihilism, one where you don't drug yourself with food, drink and sex in the face of the world being meaningless, devoid of gods and eternal values. Some would say, facing nihilism is a fine way of testing your mental reserves. So why not embrace nihilism, see it as a viable option, a place to live in and explore, all of course done with some sort of sounding board in "inner reserves," "mental energy" or whatever.

Nietzsche for his part didn't shy away from the void. He explored the essence of nihilism and atheism. "If you've dethroned God, show yourself worthy of this deed" is the theme. In the Zarathustra book it's expressed as follows, I've intimated it earlier in this chapter and here it is again:

You call yourself free? Let's hear your thoughts in principle here, and not that you escaped from slavery. Are you the one who deserved to escape it? There are many who threw away their only valuable when they threw away their servitude. Free from what? Why should Zarathustra bother? Your eyes will respond forthrightly: free for what?[51]

Personally, I've never found this supposedly God-free life so horrible. Maybe because I, in this nihilist reign, this atheist *Leitkultur* I was brought up in, still sensed that God existed. I mean, as a 17-year old to read "God is dead" in the Zarathustra book hit a nerve, this I admit. It was a statement to reflect on...! But intuitively I just got going anyway: as an agnostic, with the thesis that the death of God was not yet proven. Now, I think that God's existence is proven. He's inside me as a "Vünklein der Seele," a *soul spark* as Eckart said. The road to this realization has been instructive. Along the way, having had to live with the theory that God is dead, that good and evil doesn't exist and everything is meaningless—this has, if not strengthened me, then at least not broken me.

And today, with this idea of nihilism as a useful strategy for one who already believes in of God, this "nihilism as purification," is even more inspiring. For instance, I've met a similar thought in Simone Weil in the form of "atheism as purification" (see chapter seventeen): that by which a God believer acts *as if* God doesn't exist, a mental experiment that wipes your inner mind free for a moment, forcing you to see things in a new light. Evola's reading of Nietzsche to me has something of the same function.

No One Escapes Metaphysics

There is nothing beyond "the Beyond", Nietzsche means. All that we've expressed as transcendent values can, according to him, be reduced to the manifestations of everyday life. And the guiding principle in life is the will to power.

---

[51] Thus Spake Zarathustra, p 17, "The Way of the Creating One".

The symbol of this can be said to be the Superman (Ger. *der Übermensch*). Evola believes that Nietzsche by this made a half-measure because he just creates a new value system, a new good and evil. Good is the ambition to increase your power, evil is to reduce your power. One could imagine many other value systems than just one with the will to power as the governing principle, Evola says. If you're about to re-evaluate all values you must have your metaphysics in order and this Nietzsche has not. He throws everything overboard and says that life is all there is.

Philosophically, this isn't enough. It all makes for a materialistic, empty feedback loop. Physical life grows, flourishes and dies; what then makes the flourishing morally better than the dying? Dying for its part is a prerequisite for new life. Evola:

> Why should decadence be an evil? It is all life, and all justifiable in terms of life, if this is truly taken in its irrational, naked reality, outside any theology and teleology, as Nietzsche would have wished.[52]

Facing the fall of the transcendental world-view Nietzsche pieces together his own makeshift vision. His superman only comes forth as a homemade eschatological vision à la the forever harmonious socialist society of Marxism, established after the cataclysm of revolution. That the Superman should give all this meaning, Evola says, is a contradiction against Nietzsche's own assertion that life itself generates its meaning.

Thus Nietzsche's nihilism, as intimated by the venerable Italian, is a half-measure. A true nihilism wouldn't even have accepted the idea of the Superman. Taken on its premises, however, Nietzsche's idea of the "eternal return" is worthy of acknowledging, Evola says. That everything exists like in the Hindu *samsâra*, the eternal flow where souls are reborn into new life as a virtual school in order to develop and to ascend spiritually; this is a form of eternal return and as such is metaphysically true. Nietzsche of course didn't see it in such a refined way, he saw everything as a feedback loop; in this

---

[52] Ibid p 39.

eternal spinning around he lacked the dimension of development. However, he was on to something.

You could say: here Nietzsche approaches Being. He goes beyond mere *becoming*, beyond everyday existence, beyond mere *Seiendes* and up towards the eternal, to *Sein*. Evola considers Nietzsche to be neoplatonically viable when he in *Der Wille zur Macht* says: "For everything to return is the closest approximation of a world of becoming to a world of being."[53]

As intimated, Nietzsche here goes from *Seiendes* to *Sein*. Nietzsche's ontological, metaphysical side is always present, even though he as a rebel wanted to go against the idealism that was the *Leitkultur* of his times. As seen previously in this chapter, Abir Taha's *Nietzsche's Coming God* (2013), touches upon this, Nietzsche's esoteric tendency. His Zarathustra figure for example called himself the most pious among the ungodly. Maybe Nietzsche can be a gateway to the spiritual for the many atheists of our times.

～

The eternal return: Evola says that Nietzsche here leaves immanence and approaches the traditionalist world, a world rooted in transcendence:

> [I]t is incontestable that a confused thirst for eternity runs through Nietzsche's work, even opening to certain momentary ecstasies. One recalls Zarathustra invoking "the joy that wills the eternity of everything, a deep eternity" like the heavens above, "pure, profound abyss of light."[54]

Life and More Than Life

In chapter seven of *Ride the Tiger* Evola delves further into the metaphysical Nietzsche. In the Zarathustra book, he for

---

[53] Evola, p 40.

[54] Ibid.

example, speaks about "that which "does not say I, but *is* I".[55] To me this is a dead ringer for the "Ego sum qui sum" of the Bible. Nietzsche reached esotericism by the back door, by first denying it and then discovering it on his own, by meditating on the issues themselves. It was demonstrated above in his stumbling upon the reality of *samsâra* and the reality of reincarnation, all showing his understanding of the essence of ontology. As stated elsewhere in *Borderline* a more succinct, profound and all-encompassing aphorism than "Ego sum qui sum" doesn't exist. Even Hindus reportedly recognize that this is metaphysic's formula number one. "I am that I am" or in short, "I am," is the foundation of existence, whether the one who says it is a god or a human.

You have to crush the outer morals and re-discover it within yourself, Nietzsche seems to mean—like the eastern idea of *dharma*. You should live according to your own nature. But what is this nature? You discover it in relation to God, I figure. Freedom is to understand your limitations, and according to Kierkegaard "it is in relation to God we become what we are, free and responsible at the same time". Nietzsche for one realized that a soul should exist, even if he outwardly denied it. For "that which does not say I, but *is* I" must be seen as a person's essence, her spirit, her Self. Nietzsche seems to have put "das Selbst" as a supra individual principle, as your eternal, true Self. A strong and responsible individual in this respect can survive without a straw-man god who now has been dethroned. This person has found himself: "wie mann wird, was mann ist" (*how you become what you are*).

But since Nietzsche denies the existence of the unseen side of reality, the transcendental side, he perishes in bitterness and frustration when his power can't be directed in any specific direction. Being directed in all directions and none this superhuman will consume itself. How much better then to be a transcendentalist and realize that nothing needs to be done. "Do nothing, and everything shall be done" as Lao Tse said. This sublime tranquility Nietzsche never seems to have found. True, maybe in glimpses.

---

[55] Evola, p 41

It is in chapter eight, "Life and More Than Life", that Evola rejects Nietzsche's vitalism. You can't put life as a foundation of existence. To say that "the meaning of life is to live" may sound striking for today's lifestyle dandies, but for us with higher standards of life existence must have something more to offer. That life itself has meaning can only be said in a transcendental frame, says Evola. As stated "will to power" is just one of life's many manifestations. A life-force that according to Nietzsche just wants to surpass itself, regenerate itself, defeat itself, is just a subjective manifestation of a creature and says nothing objective about existence per se.

You could say: it's the will to life that creates desire and makes the eternal rebirth to continue; Schopenhauer essentially understood this but not Nietzsche. In this respect Nietzsche was missing the transcendental connection that Schopenhauer and Evola have. Nietzsche surrenders to desires and passions and lets them play freely in life's carousel. They tend to darken the will. Will for its part is inherently transcendentally oriented, according to the French philosopher Alain; for example there is no evil will he said. But Nietzsche for his part failed to see the difference between desire and will.

You can't just adore life, Evola says. Instead of "life" one must seek that which is "more than life". And this is done by transcendence. The eternal values are achieved "only by those in whom there is something else, and something more, than mere life."[56] As a side note, the term "mehr-als-Leben" is said to have been coined by George Simmel.

Putting Nietzsche on His Feet

Nietzsche is wrong when he calls Christianity a powerless slave morality. Instead, I figure, Christianity declares a victorious life, engendered by transcendental sources. The life-affirming

---

[56] Evola, p 50

ideals that Nietzsche praises against the perceived slave morality of Christianity, are essentially as transcendentally rooted, such as respect for the earth, life, happiness, awe, good customs and intellectual acuity.

On page 51 in *Ride the Tiger* Evola cites an unnamed ancient source that describes transcendentalism perfectly. The ascetic who has left the world behind, having cut all ties, looking inward to reach perfection, may be said to be "advancing with a devouring fire that leaves nothing behind itself." Evola congenially stresses that this spirit can also be found in Nietzsche. Nietzsche's only fault was that he stayed in the closed circle of life and therefore burned out: "[T]he fact ... that this energy remains in the closed circle of immanence and of 'life', generates a higher voltage than the circuit can sustain."[57]

But with a transcendental connection you can lift yourself from Nietzsche's Dionysian vitalism. Nietzsche's late-period thought somehow halted in the realm of the Dionysian. But it can be ennobled by Apollonian forces. As intimated, Nietzsche himself, in his early work *The Birth of Tragedy*, investigated how these two life emotions, how Apollo's bright, clear, orderly world can be supplemented by Dionysus' ecstatic, inebriated dance of life.

Evola in *Ride the Tiger* shows how a synthesis of the Dionysian and Apollonian can raise Nietzsche. Nietzsche himself was anti-spiritual but as we've seen by the studies of Safranski, Taha and Evola it's indeed possible to spiritualize this German thinker, making him a viable representative of integral esotericism.

---

[57] Evola, p 51.

20. EDITH SÖDERGRAN

In the previous chapter I spoke about Nietzsche. Now for a poet that was very much into Nietzsche: Edith Södergran (1892-1923). She took the spiritual sides of Nietzsche's thought and made them fly on the wings of music. As for Södergran the person she was ethnically Swedish. As a citizen she was the subject of the state of Finland. And I don't question that statehood. But in the following I will call her a Swede.

Edith Södergran isn't widely known outside of Finland and Sweden; being part of Finland's Swedish-speaking minority she published her poems mainly in Swedish. It's true that she once tried to push a German translation of her poems, this was in Germany in the 1920s, but effectively this came to naught.

That said, Södergran was a born poet, a poet of the Orphic kind: inspiration, grand themes, a touch of fantasy and the sky's no limit; these are prominent aspects of the Södergran style, aspects I'll here look into. There's a sense of hubris in some of these poems, there's Nietzschean approaches and attitudes. Maybe she was more Nietzschean than Nietzsche himself...? At least she carried the poetic feeling that already is to be found in *Thus Spake Zarathustra* to new levels, making the Superman philosophy really sing and dance.

For instance, Södergran has many poems on the theme of struggle, about fighting. Shimmeringly heroic, indeed mythological are lines like:

> All superstition I want to sweep out with a silent broom,
> all pettyness I will mockingly kill.
> Upon the head of The Snake I mount, stinging it with my sword.
> O you my good sword, which I have received from heaven, I kiss you.
> You shall not rest
> until the earth is a garden, where the gods dream by wonderful goblets.[58]

Lines like these are straight out of ancient times, straight out of myth and fantasy, but with a sense of urgency to it all. These aren't storybook feelings: this is real. I mean, to fight and then see the world being transformed into a divine dream: there are few other poets, in Sweden and elsewhere, who have expressed themselves so boldly. Poets normally shun the subject of praising war. War in the everyday context brings destruction and suffering. Thus it is, but it shouldn't be forbidden to write about war. Artistic freedom must have its way, like academic freedom and freedom of speech. In addition as for the poem in question, there was war in the world when this was written, the First World War drawing to a crescendo of offensive carnage. Södergran's own land, Finland, was hit by civil war in 1918.

There was a war raging and Södergran wrote about it. And she brought it to mythological heights, much like Tolkien in his trilogy mirrored World War II and made it into a timeless struggle between mythical hordes. That's it, timeless: Aragorn and Gandalf aren't bound to be seen in a WWII-context. They can forever virtually venture out into new battlefields. The movie *Arrivals* for its part sees Aragorn as Jesus and Gandalf as the Mahdi, the Twelfth Imam. So Tolkien's work can still surprise you. It was written during

---

[58] *Mystery*, from *Shadow of the Future*, 1920. This and other poems in this chapter are from Södergran's *Samlade dikter*; the English versions are mine.

WWII but doesn't exclusively reflect this.

But I digress. Edith Södergran's warlike poetry was the topic. The following poem has some everyday feel, said to have been inspired by the execution of Civil War prisoners from the Red side near her Karelian village:

> The moon knows... that blood shall flow here tonight.
> On copper tracks of the lake a certainty goes forth:
> corpses will lie among the alders on the beautiful beach.
> The moon will cast its fairest light on the strange shore.
> The wind will make its clarion call between the pines:
> How earth is beautiful in this solitary moment. [59]

The Södergran style seldom gets any more down to earth than this. Otherwise, Södergran's natural domicile is the fairy tale world. It's archetypal, timeless and mythical. Södergran's warriors sway in loose saddles, singing as they go into battle: "the spirit of song is war".

This captures the bellatorian attitude, felt and experienced by warriors from Marathon to Marsala, from Salamis to Salla. It also reminds me of Castaneda with his talk of the esotericist as a warrior, how the shamanic seeker of knowledge must have a warlike spirit, being prepared for everything. Of this I wrote in chapter 16.

Södergran dressed her war scenarios, her combat scenes in a fairy costume. There's the risk that it weakens them—the risk of making it story-bookish—but Södergran's poems are never weak or false. Here she describes a boat ride down a vortex:

> There you stand, a hero with newborn blood.
> Enraptured in tranquility, a bonfire of reflective ice,
> as if the commandment of death wasn't written for you:
> blessed waves bring your keel forward. [60]

"Enraptured in tranquility," that's a viable oxymoron for describing the warrior mindset. Possibly in the same spirit, a fairy-like style with verve, is this:

---

[59] *The Moon's Secret* from *The September Lyre*, 1918.

[60] *Vortex of Madness*, 1918.

> Mars helmets in the mist...
> Clients sitting down by overturned tables.
> Strangers rule the world...
> Higher, more beautiful, godlike.[61]

As we've seen Södergran could write in fantasy terms. But she also mentioned modern concepts, such as *Armored Trains*:

> Fifty wagons of hope I shipped to America.
> Eventually they returned, empty...
> Now I'm sending armored trains with steely masks in threatening slits:
> thousands of trailers of fulfillment return home.

Södergran's warlike side usually isn't liked by the critics. It's said to be a passing phase, the responses of a fragile mind to a stormy time. "The true" Södergran expressed herself in contemplative, quietist terms: "I found the truth in the shade of the raspberry thicket." But I would argue that her warlike creations still are viable, reflecting as they do the warrior's soul. It's as timeless as piety, motherly love, friendship, creativity, what have you. Södergran sang about all this. "The spirit of song is war" she said and this is as true as her more quietist lines.

Södergran's bellatoric poetry is warlike but, I'd say, it would not function as a soldier instruction, as a manual for war per se. But it can fire a weak soul that needs to take command of his life, who needs to live more authentically. This for instance is achieved if you know that you'll die: *memento mori*. Embodied by a soldiery role model it makes life easier to live. "Take command of your life like the captain of the ship," as sir George Trevelyan said.

Södergran by the way sang about death almost all her career—death per se, not death-in-battle or anything that warlike, which was something of a passing fancy for her during the Civil War. She had tuberculosis and knew rather early that she would die young; she was 31 when she passed away. Her death interest became a little

---

[61] *The Tempest*, 1918.

weird, this may be so, but at the same time her death poems are true and beautiful for the most part.

～

Södergran was influenced by Nietzsche. This was heartfelt, not just about being upset by the Civil War or whatever the reductionist take on this may be. Like many other contemporaries mentioned in this book, like Evola, Heidegger and Jünger (and Fröding, see the Introduction) Södergran felt compelled to take up Nietzsche's fallen mantle. And being a poet Södergran did this in an original fashion; few have caught the gist of *Thus Spake Zarathustra*, stylistically, like she has. As intimated: she was more Nietzschean than Nietzsche himself. She expressed his credo in musically true works, making her *Übermensch* poetry into a true, timeless creation.

Nietzsche's stylistic requirements we know, the introduction and other key scenes of the Zarathustra book revealing a poetic ambition that isn't always maintained in the work itself, by Nietzsche himself. You might say that Södergran, in the poetical sphere, out-Nietzsches Nietzsche. Zarathustra lectures, Södergran sings. Or, put differently: Nietzsche had poetic ambitions, he wrote poems in his youth and his poetic skills at times surfaced in Zarathustra. That said, Södergran was a poet through and through and the Nietzsche style made a lasting impression on her:

> What do I fear? I am a part of infinity.
> I am part of the immense power of The Whole,
> a lonely world within millions of worlds,
> a first-class star being the last to go out.
>
> Triumph of living, triumph of breathing, triumph of being!
> Triumph to feel the frisson of time running through your veins
> and hear the night's silent river
> and stand on the mountain under the sun.
>
> I walk on sun, I stand on sun,

I know of nothing but sun.
(...)
The sun fills my breast with sweet honey up to the brink
and she says: once all the stars go out, but they always shine
without fear.[62]

A more contemplative Nietzsche poem by Södergran is this. It's called *At Nietzsche's Grave*, the title emphasizing that the man in question was the catalyst to these lines. Södergran is a greater poet than Nietzsche, true. But one thing at a time now. Nietzsche was unique, the man with a vision of willpower again having to come to the fore. And then the disciple's words:

The great hunter is dead...
His grave I drape with warm floral curtains...
Kissing the cold stone, I say:
This is your first child in tears of joy.
Elusively I sit on your grave
as an insult—more beautiful than you ever dreamed yourself.
Remarkable father!
Your children won't fail you,
they come upon the earth in godlike strides,
rubbing their eyes: where am I?
No, really... this is my place,
this is my father's dilapidated tomb...
Gods—forever hold guard at this place.[63]

Södergran always had this Nietzschean vein. Already in the debut collection *Poems* of 1916, she said without blinking, without apologizing:

Beauty isn't the thin sauce in which writers serve themselves,
beauty is to wage war and seek happiness,
beauty is to serve higher powers.

---

[62] *Triumph to Exist* from *The September Lyre*, 1918.

[63] From *The September Lyre*, 1918.

These are lines that still stand. They go against the grain of what is now the mainstream, the fine and heartwarming, the sensitive and pitiful given in a nihilistic, non-esoteric framework. On the other hand, to be esoteric and find inspiration in the struggle of spiritual uplift, this is certainly not mainstream, *comme il faut* or allowed in today's literary salons. Therefore, we should listen to Södergran.

Södergran reminds you of another Swedish author: Karin Boye. Like her she was something of an amazon. Because they were women it wasn't demanded of them to do military service, defending their countries with weapon in hand. Thus they could relate more freely to the war mentality, less burdened by necessity. So in their poems they didn't hold back, they could give everything. Boye fought against dragons and trolls, "my death was noble and good," it was armored battle and "death and night and blood" in the Mishima sense. A man who had written this would have been labeled "war monger and violence apostle". A woman with the same repertoire didn't risk such labels.

This is one aspect of the war poetry of these women. Södergran for her part had more width than Boye, she could write poetry about everything, about women's specificity, about mountaineering, suns and stars, about the fairytale castle in the faraway wood and earth's beginning and end. She was cosmic, elementary. And one of the many elementary attitudes is the warrior's attitude and this she highlighted like no one before:

> The singers were no minstrels,
> no—gods in disguise—God's spies.
> Singers of yore—take comfort,
> good blood has flowed in your veins—
> the most abundant red warrior blood.
> The spirit of song is war.[64]

---

[64] *The Genius of the Apocalypse*, 1918.

21. T. S. ELIOT

IN THIS BOOK I've spoken about integrating opposites. Jung, Nietzsche and Södergran had the ability to cover all bases, to unite the divine with the human and the past with the present, "to boldly go where no man has gone before". In the poetry of T. S. Eliot (1888-1965) we see the same approach: East and West, tradition and modernity, the detail and the whole, everything is brought together in an eminently relatable opus.

In the poetry of T. S. Eliot everything coheres: from views on society over esotericism and spirituality to personal preferences. If Eliot makes a statement about something it reflects his whole being, society, history—everything.

You can illustrate this with a look at his esotericism. In a mature age he for example wrote the suite *Four Quartets* (1935-1942). There he delves into the depths of existence by criticizing the usual perception of time. You can't see time as linear. Instead, it's eternally present:

> Time past and time future
> What might have been and has been
> Point to one end, which is always present.

[This and other poems in this chapter is quoted from Eliot's *Collected Poems* 1909-1962.]

This has a bearing on the individual life of everyone. Like this: you can recall memories and strengthen yourself with them; having experienced happiness once this happiness lives on forever, you only have to recall it. The same applies to that which is beyond the Self, such as history. Things, events and people of the past live with us if we just remember them, cherish them and revere them. History isn't lost, it isn't forever behind us. In *Four Quartets* (part four, "Little Gidding", 1942) Eliot expresses this as follows: "History is a pattern / of timeless moments."

History is a pattern of timeless moments. We have to see the elements of the past that are timeless. And we can always access this timeless quality—by remembering, by reliving the moment, by willing the past to have a bearing on our existence. Further on in the poem this is linked to the country where Eliot lived since 1915, England. For the line continues:

> So, while the light fails
> On a winter's afternoon, in a secluded chapel
> History is now and England.

This says it all. And it is the same with Sweden, my native country. The Sweden of yesteryear is eternally present. History is now and Sweden. The Ynglinga kings, Gustav Vasa, Charles XII and their legacy will live with us if we just remember it, cherish it and nurture it.

∼

Eliot's opus is a holistic phenomenon, a *Gestalt* of esotericism and conservatism. The seldom quoted *Choruses From the Rock* (1934) are an example of this. There, in his quiet but determined way, Eliot attacks materialism and consumerism. His attitude is that of a conservative Christian, and details aside his words have power, they can also apply for the radical esotericism of today, I figure. For in that poem I note lines like this, about how "the desert grows" as Nietzsche said, the virtual desert within us (Eliot): "The desert is in the heart of your brother." Furthermore we have this criticism, how everything today is "social" while the supra-individual is forgotten: "Talking of right relations of men, but not of relations to God." Finally we are given this irony, the judgment of a civilization symbolized in its living things:

> And the wind shall say: "Here were decent godless people;
> Their only monument the asphalt road
> And a thousand lost golf balls."

As intimated *Choruses From the Rock* isn't so well known. Reportedly, it's part of a stage play. But as a text it's Eliot's most political poem: political conservatism, rooted in esotericism and Tradition. It's about faith in God as the epitome in seeing the world as something other than a venue for economic growth, party squabbles and media. Eliot gives himself God's voice in these lines to the wayward modern man, blind to the eternal values and the existence of a transcendental dimension. Today's man doesn't know what reverence is, what emotion is, what a temple is. But then you hear the voice from above saying:

> Will you build me a house of plaster, with corrugated roofing,
> To be filled with a litter of Sunday newspapers?

This poem intimates the reality of the world of Tradition, the presence of history and the reality of the invisible dimension of existence. Here is depicted how we still can search within ourselves to revive the eternal. Everything concludes with a celebration of the Perennial Light, the Light that you can't see, the Light that simply is:

> We see the Light but we see not whence it comes.
> O Light Invisible, we glorify Thee!

Thus speaks a true esotericist. Eliot incorporated his transcendental attitude in a tapestry woven of Tradition and circumspection. He was an educated gentleman in a three-piece suit but he was no bourgeois dummy. He took nothing for granted. He led poetry into new, simpler ways, free from bound form and classical motifs but still retaining a classic sounding board, uttered in allusions and quotations. In *The Waste Land* (1922) he for example intermingled everyday images from a bleak, post-war England with lines from the Upanishads, Dante and Ovid. Everything is readable and accessible, there is no rigid thesis being pushed, instead all is presented in a new aesthetic approach. The learned notes Eliot added at the end of some poems may be needed to interpret certain passages.

~

With his crony Ezra Pound (1885-1972), also an American who settled in Europe, Eliot cleaned out the debris from contemporary rhetorical poetry and revitalized it with new images, even if they in themselves were visibly banal images. It could be such as "lonely men in shirt-sleeves, leaning out of the windows," a cheap tavern with sawdust on the floor and a scene with a woman who has just received a visit from her lover and "is glad it's over."

This wasn't something you should sing about according to contemporary poetic taste. But Eliot did and he gave it all depth thanks to his classical education and his aesthetic frankness. The verse should be free, however, not total aesthetic anarchy would be the case: "No verse is free for the man who wants to do a good job," Eliot said.

~

I'm sitting here with the volume *Collected Poems 1909-1962* (Faber & Faber 1974) in front of me. This is Eliot's canonical poetic oeuvre.

Anyone interested in Eliot's so-called "spiritual development" gets it all depicted in partly enigmatic, but unmistakable terms in *Ash Wednesday* from 1930. And those who want the world's destruction painted with colors from "the dead land, the cactus land" can read *The Hollow Men* from 1925; this is nihilism but not in an exhausting, indignant way. You could say: Harry Martinson in his suite *Aniara* from 1956 depicts nihilism as defeatism: nothing works, nothing succeeds, all is doom. Eliot in *The Hollow Men* and *The Waste Land* also ventures into nihilism but on the whole has more depth than Martinson. Eliot is vaguely similar to the Evola who found energy in Nietzsche's nihilism—in the form of *active nihilism*. This I hinted at in chapter nineteen.

Eliot is a bit difficult to summarize. In the context of academic poetry, of poetry with historical depth, he could sometimes offer a laugh or two. This would be in the form of passages with rhyme in poems that are otherwise free-form, single words in French and medieval English, preambles with quotes by Heraclitus and Dante in their original language—he wasn't afraid to be called difficult and elitist, the venerable T. S. The possible inaccessibility of his writings has aesthetic motivation. Eliot's poetry is rooted in tradition but open and free.

∽

Eliot received the Nobel Prize in 1948, later on becoming something of a poetry superstar, filling football stadiums with his poetry recitals. This was quite unique in the history of literature. He also wrote light-hearted verses about cats which became the basis for the musical *Cats* by Andrew Lloyd Webber. Having ventured into popular culture one can also mention Coppola's film *Apocalypse Now* from 1979. Marlon Brando's Colonel Kurtz, reading *The Hollow Men* in his jungle temple, is a matchless scene, overwhelming in its understatement.

The main feature of Eliot's poetry is spirituality and tradition in a way you can relate to. Eliot had read his fair share of classics as well as some Indian philosophy. To make all this into poetry isn't a given thing. But Eliot could and this is what ensures his quality.

I will end this chapter by looking into the just intimated Indian strains in Eliot's poetry, unifying East and West in an integral spree. For instance we have it in "The Dry Salvages" (1941), the third of the *Four Quartets*. The poem speculates on the nature of time and here Eliot brings in some idea from Bhagavad-Gîtâ, intimated as "I sometimes wonder if that is what Krishna meant". And the idea should be that "the future is a faded song, a Royal Rose or a lavender spray / Of wistful regret for those who are not yet here to regret, / Pressed between yellow leaves of a book that has never been opened."

The future is a mere emotion. Instead, live here and now, in an eternal present and infinite now. That is what *I* figure that Krishna meant.

An exquisite incorporation of *Hindutva* in a poem spanning past and present, tradition and modernity, nihilism and faith, are the last lines of *The Waste Land*. Here Eliot manages to make poetry of a Sanskrit verb root, no mean feat. These verb roots are the condensed kernels of the Sanskrit language, a syndrome not existing in classical Sanskrit grammar but deduced from its rules. For instance, from the root *dâ* you can get words like *dâyaka*, giving, *ditsu*, wants to give, and *deshna*, gift. Eliot gives more examples, in poetic form, wishing to illustrate what we are given (*datta*), what compassion (*dayâ*/*dayadhvam*) is and how we can subdue (*damyata*, actually based on the root *dam*, to subdue) passions:

> Ganga was sunken, and the limp leaves
> Waited for rain, while the black clouds
> Gathered far distant, over Himavant.
> The jungle crouched, humped in silence.
> Then spoke the thunder
> DA
> *Datta*: what have we given?
> My friend, blood shaking my heart
> The awful daring of a moment's surrender
> Which an age of prudence can never retract
> By this, and this only, we have existed
> Which is not to be found in our obituaries
> Or in memories draped by the beneficent spider
> Or under seals broken by the lean solicitor

In our empty rooms

Eliot continues his verbal root variations with this elaboration on compassion, as intimated above:

DA
Dayadhvam: I have heard the key
Turn in the door once and turn once only
We think of the key, each in his prison
Thinking of the key, each confirms a prison
Only at nightfall, aethereal rumours
Revive for a moment a broken Coriolanus

Then finally this:

DA
Damyata: The boat responded
Gaily, to the hand expert with sail and oar
The sea was calm, your heart would have responded
Gaily, when invited, beating obedient
To controlling hands (...)

The poem has an additional passage, a lap of honor of eight lines expounding on other things. And it all ends with the words "shantih shantih shantih".

This word, *shantih*, is also Sanskrit. It means peace, quiet, tranquility, a glorified peace surpassing all conceptions of peace. It's often used in The Upanishads as a Leitmotif, as an invoker of a peaceful mood. As a closing statement for this integral poem Eliot here found *le mot propre*.

22. CASPAR DAVID FRIEDRICH

I N THIS BOOK I've delineated aspects of the Primordial Tradition (chapters 1-2 *et passim*). The perspective I've applied can be summarized as the strain of seeing the world symbolically. And a painter steeped in that tradition was the German Caspar David Friedrich (1774-1840). The concept of the *eidos*, of seeing the idea with your inner mind rather than slavishly following your outer senses, was his creed. He did paint pictures of the world around us but these images had an unmistakable *eidetic,* symbolic character.

∼

Personally, I have always liked the paintings of Caspar David Friedrich. But why? Is it because "he paints it as it is"? Or is it because he expresses a higher, hidden, esoteric reality? You can say: indeed, Friedrich depicted reality. But if so, a *dream reality*. The style may seem realistic but essentially he paints expressions of his inner mind, inner landscapes. He doesn't paint impressions of everyday reality.

This is the thesis I will discuss in this chapter. Some guidance I will get from Sten Dunér. He's a Swedish artist born in 1931, former

Professor at Konstfack in Stockholm. To the anthology *Bilderboken* (Gidlunds 1975) he contributes the essay "Caspar David Friedrich, Gud, Hitler och mamon" ("CDF, God, Hitler and Mammon"). The title is provocative, as such in sync with the revolutionary spirit of the time of publication. But on the whole Dunér makes Friedrich justice, I think. He shows us what was typical of Friedrich's paintings. On the way he also has the time to note Friedrich's role in the Third Reich (the reason for the mentioning of "Hitler" in the title). It's a fact that Friedrich was recognized by the Nazi government as a good German artist. You can also find Nazi era artwork showing a Friedrich influence.

That's how it is. But it would be narrow-minded to see Friedrich himself as a Nazi artist. From the late 1800s Friedrich has remained in the public eye, affecting diverse artistic schools. As Dunér shows Friedrich also has his appeal on modern advertising. "Back figure in desolate landscape," a person seen from behind in a deserted land, for example, is a recurrent figure in contemporary advertising images, shown by reproduced images in the Dunér essay. This is why he has "Mammon", the money god, in the title. Dunér's essay was published in the 70s but still, I'd say, the Friedrich influence on advertising is felt. This lonely figure seen from behind, placed in a heroic landscape—this is Western Man, the Faustian Spirit, and with Friedrich having given us the template, the iconographic pattern, this image lives on in magazine adverts and such. We even saw this back figure in Third Reich art, like "Sentinel by the Sea" by Lünstroht (1942).

But I won't go into these derivations and deviations in this chapter. This is about esotericism in art, Friedrich-style. And a recurring sub-theme of Dunér's essay is the "supra-real," dreamlike quality of Friedrich's art. Dunér is a prudent general, he doesn't anchor his interpretation in esotericism (as I do), but he certainly gives pointers in this direction. "God" in the essay title after all takes the argument into the realm of the transcendental. And what I want to point at is this: Friedrich can't be reduced to a painter depicting everyday reality, nor to an inflexible maker of allegories. For allegory, you can maybe say that "the evergreen fir trees" in Friedrich's art is a symbol of "the hope of the pious man". The quoted words reflect Friedrich's own thoughts, rendered in a discussion of the religious painting *The Tetschen Altar.* Pines and conifers undoubtedly have formal symbolic qualities but you can't reduce it into a rigid pattern. Dunér doesn't exactly say that but he broadens the discussion on Friedrich's art from being more than just about allegories.

As hinted Dunér shows us the elements of Friedrich's art that he was alone of, at least in the time this German was active. And it was about painting pictures of a higher, dreamlike reality. *The Abbey in the Oakwood* 1810, for example, is not the image of any existing ruins. Friedrich has composed the whole from his inner mind. Contributing to the dreamlike atmosphere is for example the absence of background. Normally Western artists compose their pictures à la foreground, middle-ground and background. This may, for its part, be seen as the Faustian draw towards the horizon as Spengler mentioned, the expression of the distinctive way of life here in the West, first visible in Renaissance paintings and then in the works of Dutch and German masters, and in pictures by Claude Lorrain and all, expressing the restless *Plus Ultra*, the constant "ever onwards, westward ho"-spirit of western man.

The artists of the early modern age discovered the horizon. And even in Friedrich's more customary nature pictures, there is a horizon. But here, in his picture of the ruined abbey, there is no horizon. And that's the defining character of this picture. Dunér:

> This picture (...) is neither a sentimental mood painting or a sober landscape. It has a deeper meaning (...) [Dunér then recounts various interpretations, of which I think Jens Christian Jensen's is the best:] *Jensen* demonstrates that the formal structure of the picture reveals that the artist's aim must have been to express something symbolically. The foreground suddenly disappears behind the ruin. Everything disappears beyond a vague and impermeable imaginary wall: the room ceases. Fully unmediated emerges the bright sky. The monks are walking into an immeasurable darkness. Two sonnets of the contemporary poet Theodor Körner are about

this monastery, and in them are clearly marked a religious-metaphysical meaning.⁶⁵

There seems to be nothing to add. To interpret the image politically etc. (this has also been made. Dunér reproduces such thoughts) to me seems fruitless. *The Abbey in the Oakwood* is a compelling symbolic dream image.

Dunér also says a lot about the Friedrich painting *The Wanderer Above the Mists* (*Der Wanderer über dem Nebelmeer*, 1817-1818). Here he concentrates on the fact that it's a back view. Friedrich has painted a number of them: a human turning his back to us occupying the center of the image (such as *Frau vor der untergehenden Sonne* and *Zwei Männer den Mond betrachtend*).

This phenomenon is of interest, but I'll bypass it here. What interests me with *Der Wanderer*...is that this too is a supra-real symbolic painting, an image created out of something seen in the artist's interior. This purpose—I suppose—is to show the titanic sublimity, the Nietzschean tranquility you feel when you've climbed a mountain. The image seems to be anticipating Nietzsche's hikes in Sils-Maria as well as the Nietzsche-influenced Julius Evola's spiritual climber passion.

To note here is the simplicity of the execution of the painting. Technically, this isn't very advanced. The mountains in the distance have the characteristics of a backdrop and the middle-ground only seems to consist of power lines directing everything towards The Hero. Friedrich has been criticized for his seemingly simple brushwork (for example by a certain von Ramdohr).⁶⁶ But as Dunér shows us this criticism is misplaced. I agree: if you paint dream heavy, primal scenes, then it's the symbolic power of the motif that shall convince you, not, for example, coloristic finesse to give the illusion of light, with highlights and shadow à la Titian, Vermeer, Constable, etc. Friedrich's paintings may give you some everyday realistic feeling because of the shadows that indeed are there (like the rocks the heroic mountain climber is standing on),

---

⁶⁵ Dunér, p 77-79, translated into English by LS.

⁶⁶ Dunér, p 61.

but essentially Friedrich's most important works are pictures of dream states, not everyday scenes from a certain time of day.

Friedrich's pictures are simple but not simplistic. Incidentally, I am struck by the number of heavyweight artists having made art that is "simple," that is, technically relatively easy to perform. For instance, Bengt Liljegren (*Pink Floyd*, Historiska Media 2010) says that Pink Floyd's "psychedelic" songs in general aren't technically difficult to execute. A normally skillful rock musician can quite easily interpret the songs. I also think of the seeming simplicity of many stories of Poe and Borges. To sum up: *simple* is not the same as *simplistic*.

∼

Now let's look at Friedrich's *The Stages of Life* (*Die Lebensstufen*, 1834). This painting has something of a contrived feeling. It's been designed, not to give us a suggestive, ambiguous dream scene, but to show us something by way of allegory. Allegories aren't the mainstay of high art but I like this picture anyway, it has a certain indescribable feeling in spite of the learned undertext. It summarizes life—all of our lives—in an unmistakable way. According to a common interpretation (Gradmann, Börsch-Supan) the ships match the figures on the beach: the old man with the cane is matched by the big ship next to the beach, symbolizing a life journey close to its end. The two children are symbolized by the two small boats near the beach: their life voyage has just begun. And the man and the woman, the middle aged parents of the children, are represented by the two large ships in the distance, fully occupied with sailing the sea of life.[67]

I think this sums up the picture quite well. And like Dunér I note how the image in addition to this has an indefinable atmosphere. It's a masterpiece, pure and simple. A timeless classic, beyond labels such as romanticism, symbolism, etc. It's both dreamlike and realistic, both symbolic and a scene of everyday.

Now for a look at *The Cross on the Mountain* (*Kreuz im Gebirge*). Dunér mentions an earlier version of this image (*Tetschen*

---

[67] After Dunér, p 94.

Altar) and gives us interpretations which say that it's essentially a dream vision, a symbolic-esoteric image, taking it beyond being an image of something real. Indeed, in the Catholic South Germany you can see such crucifixes set along trails and roads. So it has the quality of everyday reality but this isn't the whole story. *Kreuz im Gebirge*, sporting a crucifix in a mountain scenery with a gothic cathedral as backdrop, is a dream scene.

As for the bare facts of this painting: the crucifix of the painting doesn't depict the crucified Christ himself. It's a picture of an artifact so the basic premise for the image has a slight everyday character. But by simplifying the picture elements Friedrich has brought it all to a higher level. My personal impression is: this is symbolism par preference. We all understand that it's stylized and "made up," this view of a church gable flanked by trees and with the crucifix in the middle foreground. But despite the arranged nature of the picture the overall result is very poignant, a symbolically saturated painting that signals tradition and spirituality within a Nordic way of life, the last thing conveyed by the conifers and the rustic forest environment. The icing on the cake is the divine light illuminating the scene from above. And once again we see how the painting technique itself isn't very advanced. It's relatively simple. But as hinted, this is not the same as simplistic. "It is just right."

∼

All told, Friedrich was an esoteric artist. And he himself was quite clear about esotericism as an artistic strategy. He said, among other things: "The painter shouldn't just paint what he sees before him, but also what he sees within him."[68]

As for Friedrich's genius as a "painter of a dream reality," there were few of his contemporaries who saw it. True, he was comparatively acclaimed for a while, but towards the end of his life realism, uttered in the intimate rusticity of the Düsseldorf School, became all the rage in Germany. Then, towards the end of the 1800s, Friedrich's opus was rediscovered by the Swiss painter

---

[68] Quoted from Dunér, p 68.

Arnold Böcklin (1827-1901).

Böcklin took up the style of "after the inner mind composed dream images in seemingly realistic style". For example his *Toteninsel* (1880) clearly shows this: a white figure is brought to a red sandstone island of cypresses and white temples, the surrounding sea an absinthe green. This is stylistically and conceptually inconceivable without the influence of Friedrich. The direct inspiration to *Toteninsel* Böcklin is said to have gotten from the burial island of San Michele in the Venice lagoon, a walled island with cypresses visibly sticking up above the top of the wall. This island is flat and fairly square but Böcklin's vision is something completely out of the dream world. In other words, a "dream reality" in the spirit of Caspar David Friedrich.

23. INTEGRAL ARTISTRY

Is it possible to formulate an esoteric theory of art? Possible or not, this is what I'm trying to do in this chapter. It's in sync with the integral theme of this book. It's about art as an integration of opposites, a uniting of contraries. In short, it's about *integral artistry.*

Harmony Through Conflict

To summarize what I'm proposing in this chapter, I would like to say: *art is the striving for harmony through conflict.* In order to reach artistic harmony you have to stage a conflict of some kind—like the individual versus the collective, action versus contemplation, male versus female, East versus West etc.

The impulse to this idea per se, this way of looking at art, is from the concept of "The Seven Rays," for instance discussed by Alice Bailey (1880-1949). This is an esoteric way of structuring the different moods, attitudes and energies of man, and the fourth ray in this system is that of the artist. And the motto for him was, indeed, "harmony through conflict".

This is my starting point in defining what art is. What is the specificity of art, what distinguishes it from science and politics?

"Harmony through conflict" may be part of the answer. Science is about finding truth and politics is about priorities. And art is about harmony—through conflict.

We can illustrate this with Judas Priest, the British hard rock band. Their very name sums up this phenomenon, of "harmony through conflict". On the site "The Judas Priest History"[69] there is a Rob Halford quote from 1983. The band leader says that the band name has been good to them because it symbolizes the music, showing that they

> [...] can put across music that is very, very heavy and powerful and sinister in one respect, but also we can lighten up (and I use the word loosely) with the other types of music, such as the "Beyond the Realms of Death" or the "Dreamer Deceiver", the "(Take These) Chains" off...those mellower sides of the band. So I think the two words intermingle—the Judas and the Priest, the good and the bad, the light and the shade.

Holistic Aesthetics

This is the unique mix, the concept making Judas Priest so great, defining the group's specificity: the mix of light and shade. Lyrically and musically they give us the whole gamut, the whole spectrum from ecstasy and tasty climes to elevated hymns and pathos. The best Judas Priest records strike a balance between the "Judas" and the "Priest" elements—and, conversely, the not so great albums tend to have too much of the one, like *Turbo* being to heavy on the light element and *Painkiller* too heavy on the dark.

But overall, Judas Priest symbolizes a unique mixture of light and shade, sometimes in single songs, like "Thunder Road," "Exciter" and "Ram It Down". As for the more sombre tunes we have "Sinner," "The Sentinel" and "Killing Machine" and as for

---

[69] http://www.jugulator.net/judas_priest_history.htm

anthem-like, uplifting tunes we have "Solar Angels," "You Don't Have To Be Old To Be Wise," "United" and "Red, White and Blue".

To make my point: any rock group, or singer, or artist in general, who manages to fuse light and shade, black and white, good and bad; who can give us tributes to carnal pleasures along with spiritual hymns, both of them sincerely meant—this artist is a true artist. Just think of Shakespeare (comedies and tragedies, light and dark realms, it's all there in the opus), Goethe (elevated gnomic and romantic poetry along with Faust going off with Mephistopheles, the Devil's right hand) and Homer both depicting the elevated Olympic realms and the shady climes of Hades. And why not the film *The Third Man* (1949), juxtaposing a scene in a Ferris wheel, giving us a bird's view of Vienna, with a scene in the sewers, a secular Underworld.

In the true artwork both light and dark are along, conducting a coexistence. And as an advice to the budding artist, I'd say, don't expressly try to mix them in the same scene, in the same line, in the same breath. Explore the possibilities of each mood at its proper place. This, for its part, is one of many aesthetic tips Ingmar Bergman (1918-2007) delivers in his autobiography *Laterna Magica* (1987).

Structure = Freedom

The theory of art here displayed has just examined the nature of the artwork itself. But the process of making art, to create – how is this done? Of this I say the following. To create optimally *you have to establish a structure within which you can be free.*

I originally got this aspect from a description of Elvis Presley and his musical project, how his accompanying musicians drew from diverse styles in order for Elvis to perform optimally: they created a structure within which Elvis could be free. The Led Zeppelin ideal of "tight but loose" also describes this. Musically, this means for the group in question: there's a lot of riffing and showing off going on along with more airy attitudes. There's the solid drumming of John Bonham along with Jimmy Page's playful outings on the guitar. But it also applies to the lyrical content, with Luciferianism and "a whole lotta love" along with more spiritual love ballads, "Down by the Seaside," "In the Light" and the pure artistic joy of "The Song Remains the Same".

See the Light

These were the main points of my artistic theory. Below are some informal notes on "how to create," some artistic notions I've gathered over the years with a focus on the art-form I've personally specialized in, literature.

"Forget color and form, try to see the light!" By itself light can give shape and color to a picture. This was the philosophy of Swedish painter Ivan Augéli (1869-1917). This could be a motto for any artist, even for writers. Trying to see the essential around you, not being enmeshed in programs.

As I mentioned in the chapter on acting (chapter sixteen), SF author E. E. Smith had a problem writing synopses. He discovered that it was hard if not impossible to delineate in a few pages all the things a novel was going to say. Instead, the mere act of writing the novel tends to realign the intended plot and open up new vistas. "On s'engage et puis on verra" as Napoleon said, which I discussed in the same chapter. Even artists should remember this. After some formal preparations, get going and then ponder the material. You can't outline all of a novel beforehand.

As I writer of novels I can vouch for this. I've never written any synopses. I'd say: writing beforehand summaries is an excuse for not writing. Rather, invest that energy in something tangible, like writing a first draft of a scene.

This is akin to another aspect I mentioned in the action chapter (sixteen), an aspect in line with the above, namely, that of the test pilot having to take the prototype aircraft for a test flight. Sometime you reach that point where no more preparations can be made. You just have to do it, get going. This could make you think of a mathematical point said to exist in the context of crime investigations: *Borkmann's Point*, once mentioned by Swedish crime writer Håkan Nesser (1950-). In gathering information about a case, this Borkmann Point is the point beyond which any more added info rather clouds than clarifies the matter. So in light of the above, when preparing for a novel there comes a time when further research or formal preparations don't help you in writing the book; on the contrary, it drags it downs.

Get Going

As for research per se in novel writing, I am of the opinion that it shouldn't be done at all—beforehand. If needed it can be done afterward, after having done the main part of the writing. The hardest part in novel writing is to make lively scenes and this can to 99% be done with the help of your imagination. Then, let's say, if you've written about a marble hall and that this, in view of the novel taking place in 15th century Japan, is historically inconsistent— well then, change it to "the correct masonry" after having done research—but only then.

Strictly from a creative, artistic point of view, doing research is like writing synopses: an excuse for not writing.

But of course, some concept of what you're going to write is needed before you get going. Don't rely to heavy on imagination and improvisation as means. The previously mentioned Ingmar Bergman, in *Laterna Magica*, also maintained that "only the prepared can improvise". This is related to what I mentioned earlier in this chapter, exemplifying it with Elvis, of the artistic process as "establishing a structure within which you can be free". A structure is needed for spontaneity and improvisation to blossom.

24. SWEDENBORG

EMANUEL SWEDENBORG (1688-1772) was a Swedish esotericist. His followers call his doctrine "Swedenborgianism". He himself called it "the true Christian religion". Personally I'd call it *Perennialism*. Essentially Swedenborg's creed is well in sync with the metaphysical world-view of Plato, Plotinus, Goethe, Jünger and other thinkers I've highlighted in this book.

Materialist Beginnings

Curiously enough, Emanuel Swedenborg didn't start out as an esotericist. In the beginning of his scientific career he was a materialist bent on finding "the location of the soul within the body," like searching for the cellular processes that occur when thinking. This typical reductionism we need not here concern ourselves with. But the interested can read about Swedenborg's reductionism and mechanism in Sten Dunérs *Världsmaskinen* (*The World Machine*, 2004).

In time Swedenborg became a spiritualist and an esotericist, "the Columbus of the spirit world". And he did indeed tell about some spectacular travels in the higher realms. But as for the ontological system on which Swedenborg based his interpretations of his spiritual experiences, from the perspective of idealism and "theosophy" (theosophy in the wider sense), then Swedenborg is a dyed-in-the-wool Perennialist. Swedenborg maintains that the world essentially is of a spiritual, non-material nature. And this many have argued before him. Swedenborg is the foremost Swedish mystic but he didn't start from scratch. He knew idealist thinkers like Plato, Aristotle, Plotinus, Augustine, Descartes and Leibniz.

Bergquist

A biographer labeling Swedenborg a theosophist in this sense, is Lars Bergquist (1930-). Himself a Christian Bergquist shows a rather fine understanding of Swedenborg's teachings. Swedenborg is part of the opinion that there is one God and that divine grace, compassion and reality flows down and procures an influence (Latin *influxus*) in humans. Man has light within himself and is both attracted to God and to the material, everyday sphere. According to Bergquist, Swedenborg teaches that man has both Divine Love within him as well as a stroke of evil. Man is a battlefield susceptible for influences. Man has a free will; he can accept or reject the concept of being one with God, of having a spark of the Eternal Light within him.

Bergquists's Swedenborg biography is called *Swedenborgs hemlighet* (*Swedenborg's Secret*). It was published in Swedish in 1999. It covers its subject from all aspects on its 560 pages. However, a 200 page essay by Olof Lagercrantz—*Dikten om livet på den andra sidan* (1996; the title means, *The Poem About Life on the Other Side*) gives a more apt picture of the, shall we say, Borderline character of Swedenborg's work, adding an artistic aspect to it. Swedenborg was no poet but Lagercrantz was, and reading Swedenborg's opus as a poem helps him to uncover some peculiar sides of it.

Apparently Lagercrantz (1911-2002) has read most of what Swedenborg has written, particularly he has plowed through the rather monotonous prose of *Arcana Caelestica* which was the magnum opus. And here and there, interspersed in Swedenborg's elaborations, he has found treasures, more personal reflections that Swedenborg condescended to during his teaching of what the hidden meaning of the Bible is.

The Text

Lagercrantz in his work has a rather clever approach. It isn't psychological and reductionist, this has been done before, and it isn't theological or even esoteric. Lagercrantz instead reads Swedenborg as a text. Being schooled in "The New Criticism" of the 1940s Lagercrantz has a keen eye for the essential. Therefore, the author's person is put out of focus, his quirks and intentions being neglected. Instead, the text speaks. Lagercrantz thus avoids the question that is often asked by researchers: was Swedenborg crazy? Are his texts either a) completely true or b) completely fabricated? Lagercrantz takes no position on Swedenborg's mental health. He sees *the text* and infers a few things from it.

For example, Lagercrantz describes Swedenborg's idea of "the universe as a human being". The shape of the Cosmos is that of a man, "the great man"—Homo Magnus. Lagercrantz calls this complex of Swedenborg's thought his "boldest poem". Personally, I wouldn't call it mere poetry. Homo Magnus is an established idea in Perennialism. Even Krishna worshipers maintain the thought. Krishna in his *virât-rûpa* is incorporating the whole Cosmos. Lagercrantz for his part does what he can to render this idea, in Swedenborg's conception of it, understandable for the common reader; I'll lift my hat to that.

Lagercrantz takes us into the divine thought of Swedenborg. Like showing us the idea of how God never turns away his face from anyone. And of course never throwing anyone into hell. God is sheer mercy and acceptance. It's man himself who turns away from God, man himself who chooses evil. This Swedenborg formulated as: (Latin): "Deus non transferat hominem, sed homo se ipsum" ("God doesn't deliver man [to heaven or hell], this the man himself does").

This is the Perennial, and modern, esotericist world-view. The idea of a judgmental God has nothing to do with the spiritual mindset. I know that materialists and nihilists like to accuse the esoteric faction for this, for adhering to a vengeful God—but essentially, for this they accuse us in vain.

Dream Diary

Lagercrantz's Swedenborg essay makes him understandable to the artistically minded everyman. The same goes for Swedenborg's *Dream Diary*. It was written in the 1740s when the materialist, positivist Swedenborg had a religious crisis. These notes were never meant for publication. But in time they have become a classic of its own: a portrait of a man, alone with God, the Universe and the disturbing visions of his dreams.

The Dream Diary is the most readable of Swedenborg's books. It gives us glimpses of everything: beauty, horror, piety. The dreams in themselves made Swedenborg realize that searching for the soul in the physical body was futile. Instead he would become a spiritual Columbus, mapping the vistas of the astral world.

25. ERNST JÜNGER

ERNST JÜNGER (1895-1998) was an informal teacher of esotericism. He acknowledged the existence of eternal forms, of a higher order affecting the everyday world. Throughout all his career, from *Der Arbeiter* in 1932 to the late diary (last volume 1995) he gave his readers central aspects of German idealism, of the concept of *Urbilder*, essence and form.

Eumeswil

Ernst Jünger knew how to make idealism understandable to the educated everyman. For instance, in the novel *Eumeswil* (1977) he showed us what a Gestalt is. Like this: the teacher Vigo speaks about a pine tree having had its top broken off in a snowstorm. Then, which can be seen in nature, a side branch may assume the role of trunk, growing in an upward, soon enough perpendicular direction. The form of the tree is re-established. What, then, Vigo asks the narrator, Manuel Venator, shall we call this? Manuel says: I'd call it *the restitution of the Gestalt through das Urbild*.

This is very concise and clarifying as for the nature of *die Urbilder*. And it shows that this concept, *Urbild*, still has a place in modern science. What gives the tree its shape? Its particular *Urbild*.

Jünger Bio

I've written a biography on Jünger. It's called *Ernst Jünger – A Portrait* (Manticore Press 2014). In this study I summarize what Jünger says about esoteric symbolism in *Eumeswil*. In sync with the Plotinian doctrine he makes the existence of *die Urbilder* tangible: no need to dream of a distant world of ideas since all its marvels are manifested in the everyday world: "No transcendence is needed, everything is revealed here and now. Trust your senses. Goethe said that and Jünger reminds us of it."[70]

This idea is formulated by Jünger as, "das Urbild is Bild und Spiegelbild." This untranslatable German line would mean: the original image is both transcendent and immanent. Like I said in the biography:

> Idealism for its part is about recognizing the idea. And the ideal form is copy and original at the same time: "das Urbild is Bild und Spiegelbild" as the German original of "Eumeswil" has it. The transcendental image or idea is copied in the everyday object, living on in the copy as well as being transcendent. It's immanent and transcendent at the same time. This we have from Plotinos, elaborating and refining the Platonian philosophy of mere transcendence. (...) Everything is guided by its innermost essence, by its idea, the things existing for the ideas to have something to show themselves in. The idea is what makes the objects, the flowers, animals, everything, live, visible in any garden, forest or whatever. Jünger dedicates some pages in this novel to bring this argument home.[71]

---

[70] Svensson, p 218.

[71] Ibid.

War Diary

In my Jünger bio I discussed some further Jüngerian esotericism. Like what he says in his War Diary. The following touches upon subjects treated in this book, *Borderline*, so I'll give it to you without comment:

> The Jünger war diary is replete with Jüngerian idealism, differing in style if not content from Cambridge Platonism and German Idealism. As I've already said: Jünger brings us the metaphysics of everyday, making the abstractions of idealism tangible for the common man. Like for instance: what's in the chessboard king? In this, Jünger says, the magic of the archaic kingdom is preserved, the chess piece in question being a discreet symbol of a lost world. The same goes with hunting trophies: they are no simple wall decorations, they are carriers of magic power, talismans there to accumulate happiness and life force, mana, for the hunter. Even artists may need talismans like these, like the painter Braque whom Jünger met in Paris on October 4, 1943, his studio being graced with certain objets d'art that weren't motifs to be painted but rather magical objects assembling artistic mana. Jünger looks at everyday objects decoding their meaning. For instance oil in a barrel is dark but a spilled out drop is a psychedelic palette, this being due to its thinness [Kirchhorst, November 5, 1945]. The thinner the more etheric. It's like Goethe said tangible-intangible (Ger. "sinnlich-übersinnlich"), living on the edge between the material and the immaterial. The war diary also says that the way to the Southern Paradise can be found by maps, but a better way is to let oneself be guided by images of opulence and riches, of grapes ripening in the sun and the like [Kirchhorst, September 16, 1945]. This to me is a simple and striking example of Jünger's symbolic world view.[72]

---

[72] Svensson, p 218-219.

Symbolic World-view

Jünger's esoteric mindset is mapped in a study by Gisbert Kranz: *Ernst Jüngers symbolische Weltschau* (1968). This is the book for the student in need of a systematic look into Jünger's symbolic world-view. But in essence it's the same pattern that I've delineated here: the primeval images—*Urbilder*—are represented in Symbols, and so on and so forth. One of the discussions in Kranz's book is the notion that almost all of Jünger's book titles are symbolic, like *The Worker, The Adventurous Heart, On the Marble Cliffs, The Glass Bees* and the city names *Eumeswil* and *Heliopolis*. All his work have a symbolic character, all the titles intimating their *Gestaltkvalität*.

God

Jünger once said: "The divine existence is eternal presence. And life only exists where the divine is present."

This might represent his theistic side. In his writing Jünger acknowledged God and the divine. Conversely, he warned against atheism. In *Eumeswil* and the late diary (*Siebzig Verweht*, 1965-1996) he highlighted the current, prevailing atheism as an ill of the times. To merely stop seeing a higher metaphysical dimension in reality is sick.

Jünger saw the presence of the divine in the everyday, he saw the *eidos* in the ephemeral objects. He was an informal teacher of esotericism and this aspect of him I wanted to elevate in my bio. Because, all the other English language biographies on Jünger ignored this (q.v. Neaman, Nevin).

26. THE ESOTERIC WORLD-VIEW

BORDERLINE IS AN inquiry into things metaphysical. In Perennial fashion I've examined the foundation of existence itself. What is the true nature of Being, of Esse, of *Sein*? In this book I've tried to answer this question from different angles. Hereby a kind of summary of the esoteric mindset—not expressly of what has been said page by page in this book, but overall. This is The Esoteric World-View I and many Perennial thinkers adhere to. This is The Esoteric World-View that mankind needs now, to meet the moral, ontological, mental and astral challenges ahead.

Reality Is Spiritual

The basic assumption of The Esoteric World-View is that reality is of a spiritual, non-material nature. Matter is of a lower reality than ideas, thoughts, patterns and models. Matter is darkness, disorder and chaos; order is light, form and harmony.

In *The Emerald Tablets of Thoth* we gather the wisdom: "as above, so below". Which means: the structure of the microcosm is in accordance with the structure of the macrocosm. The macrocosm is the Universe, the microcosm is Man. What, then, does man consist of? I sketched a similar survey of the *subtle bodies* in chapter twelve. Hereby a kind of repetition. Taking it from the bottom, man first consists of the Physical Body. Closely adhering to the physical body is the Etheric Body, sustaining it with life. The next level is the Astral Body or Emotional Body, being the place for emotions, dreams and feelings. The next level is the Mental Body, being the place for thoughts, the intellect, the mind. Next we have the True Self (Sanskrit Âtman, or in Rudolf Steiner's terminology, der *Atemselbst*), sometimes called "the Spirit".

The Etheric, Astral and Mental bodies are the "subtle bodies" of man. They aren't literally "levels," they are ever subtler bodies enclosing the physical body, each one permeating the "lower," less real bodies.

That was ontology from the human, microcosmic aspect. Further, if we see things from a macroscopic point of view, a view mirroring the microcosm like Thoth pointed at, then we see this. The material Cosmos is earth, the planets, the galaxies. Above them (or rather, spiritually-dimensionally beyond) are higher levels. Does for instance earth have a soul? Yes, esoteric theory makes that postulation. Mother Earth is the name of the soul of the Earth, also known as Erda, Gaia or "the ecosystem". The higher levels in this model have ever more complex beings as the essence of things—angels, archangels etc.—and above them all is the Causal Sphere, the World of Ideas. Above this is God, the Absolute Consciousness.

This is the esoteric theory on which my thought is based. This is the esoteric model of Man and the Cosmos laying the formal, metaphysical base for the *Borderline* discussions. I've already intimated most of it in this book: God is the Primeval Light and Man's soul is a spark of that light. If man acknowledges his Inner Light then he unites with God. The goal of our earthly existence is to learn this lesson until we can unite more permanently with God, not needing to go through the chain of birth and rebirth any more, being free from the confluence of *samsâra*.

And even if it's risky to slip into programmatic passages like this ("we have to do this and that") it's got to be done somehow. I mean, of course science, including ontology, has to be performed as objectively as possible. This is the constant scientific ideal, both for the humanities and natural science. But man can no longer create intellectual systems where the *Sein* of man is left out of them. We're all *Seiendes im Sein*. No one can think himself out of Sein, no one can theoretically place himself above or beyond it.

Order From Above

Reality is spiritual in nature. This I've tried to show you. What is of essence here is this: *that order always comes from above*. Higher, more complex levels affect the lower. True, according to Plotinos there is also a flow back through the levels, from lower to higher; the system isn't rigidly set on a one-way flow. But generally reality is structured from higher to lower, symbolized in the concept of *thought creates the brain, not the other way around*. This esoteric idea is advocated by Balogh (1999), as I've shown earlier in this book. Specifically in chapter 5.

The material objects have the shape they have because of their inherent, immaterial pattern. No material objects can emerge spontaneously. Nothing comes spontaneously out of the material world—but spontaneously something comes to it. Spontaneously the material level can be affected by the spiritual realm.

As humans, we are who we are because of our souls—because of our souls' karmic baggage and how these souls will best be educated on the journey of life. As for the inanimate things, they have their shape because of their *eidos*, their conceptual, forming element. This latter phenomenon is familiar to everyone who has heard of Plato and Aristotle. A globe, for instance (a football, a pinball, a tennis ball), looks the way it does because it's sharing the eternal idea of the sphere.

This is merely a sketch giving you the outline of the metaphysical world-view. The ethic of the future has to be based in a spiritual, higher order. Conversely, a materialist ethic (Sartre's existentialism, Dewey's pragmatism, Bentham's utilism, logical positivism, diverse examples of "intellectualism") is an ethic with no serious ontological, esoteric foundation at all, a creed approaching disorder, darkness and despair. An attitude approaching The Chaotic Mindset (q.v. chapter 17).

In *Borderline* I've intimated a creed of Integral Esotericism, stressing Holism, unity between an individual's Inner Light with the Primeval Light and existence in the Here-and-Now—a doctrine of order and harmony, pointing to a glorious future for us all. Contrariwise, the current nihilist materialism of the West is a decadent doctrine. I don't think that a random nihilist is an evil operator out to destroy. But there has to be a shake-up of the intellectual discussion. Ontology, esotericism and speculative metaphysics of the Plotinos, Jung, Jünger and Goethe kind must again be taken seriously. Science can no longer treat the Question of Reality as a non-issue. Philosophy is about challenging everything, even nihilist reductionism. The attitude of "ignoring the problem and hoping that it will go away" is futile.

Energy

Hereby some words on *energy* from an existential point of view. This section touches on things said before in *Borderline*, and in some cases brings in a new perspective. We all need energy to live. And we all know that food and drink provides us with the energy to keep our physical bodies going. But there are more subtle forms of energy than the chemical energy received from daily nutrition. Energy can be of a more or less organized type. It's like with high voltage energy; this needs to be transformed from 10.000 Volts to 220 in order to be of use to everyday man. And as an esotericist it's close at hand to see high voltage energy as a simile to God and lower voltage energy as the energy level where man exists.

In the Esoteric, Holistic Paradigm everything is life, everything is energy. The Universe is a unified organism, a super-being pulsating with Divine Energy. As individuals we're all part of this unfathomable, superior Ur-Energy, on the top levels an energy of high potential and high frequency, and then converted to lower frequencies and voltages to the lower ontological levels.

The divine energy is manifested in different forms, all the way from the Causal Sphere down to stars and our own sun and earth and then in individual beings such as ourselves. Each individual has an amount of energy, an energy being part of the Primeval, Divine Energy.

Flame of Inspiration

Everything in the Universe is connected, everything is energy. God is energy, man by way of his spirit is energy. All separate entities are energy, even the inanimate objects. Remember the formula $E=MC2$, "energy equals mass times the speed of light to the power of two". Everything is energy, even the tiniest speck of dust; there are no lifeless objects, and there is no space devoid of energy, forcefields or particles. "The perfect vacuum" is a mere theoretical concept.

Speaking of modern physics, this has also learned us that *energy can't be destroyed, it can only change form*. This is the principle of the conservation of energy, there to be used as a "natural science proof of God" if you so choose.

Everything is energy. What, then, is the spiritual concept of energy? It can be formulated in the following way. The individual, having hopes and dreams, having the inspiration to do this and that, is an example of energy. And this energy isn't solely derived from food and drink, from chemical sources; it's derived from higher levels, from Divine Realms. And since this section has a morally prescriptive inclination, a bias toward "how to act," then the question is: how do you act as an individual to "get energy," how do you keep the Flame of Inspiration burning, how do you keep going in the noisy confusion of life, having the energy to do what you do?

I have some rules of thumbs for this. For instance, in *The Power of Silence* Don Juan says to Castaneda: "[W]hat you're learning is how to save energy."[73] This is a neutral, pragmatical way of looking at your conduct of life. When doing this and that, does it deplete me of energy or does it give me energy, replenishing my energy source? For instance, we talk today about how this and that "sucks energy". And that is an excellent way of deciding what areas of interest to pursue and what to avoid. It also tells us of what people, attitudes and syndromes to avoid and what people, attitudes and syndromes to seek, nurture and encourage.

Attitudes sucking energy are these: irony, sarcasm, *Schadenfreude* of the systemic, habitual kind; passive nihilism, apathy, feeling weak, feeling helpless, acting condemnatory. In short, sporting a Chaotic Mindset (q.v. chapter 17).

Attitudes giving you energy are these: harmony, balance, exerting compassion, being constructive (both virtually and by constructing tangible objects), the idea of keeping order around you and doing it in an equanimous spirit. In short, adhering to *Seinsphilosophie* and employing Integral Esotericism.

It's harder than it seems to get going on the energetic lifestyle, at least for one being in the claws of negativism. And you don't have to be a saint in order to be energetic. But a change of attitude is needed for the person who is constantly drained of energy and not realizing that he can change this order of things by his own willpower. It's merely about leaving the quarrelsome websites, avoid persons who are "energy thieves" and instead start acting and thinking constructively.

Ontological Hierarchy

Earlier in this chapter I elaborated on the concept of essential reality being of a higher order than material, everyday reality. I've also said it previously in this book. For instance, I've maintained that "thought creates the brain, not the other way around" (chapters

---

[73] Castaneda, 1987, p x-xi.

two and five). Another way of saying it is that if there's a pot there has to be a potter. The pot doesn't magically take shape "of itself". The phenomena causing the pot are primarily of an immaterial nature: the idea of making a pot taking shape in the head of the potter, the design he chooses and the way he takes the lump of clay and forms it with his hands.

Higher affects lower, not the other way around. You can't deduce the form of a rose, a lion or a horse from the periodic system. A rose gets is shape from an idea in the Causal Sphere, not from inorganic matter.

Reductionist science makes the most stupendous claims. Man is supposed to have developed "of himself," out of nothing? A self-conscious creature with amazingly complex organs like the eye and the brain—out of nothing...? This simile was once proposed by a wise man: to say that man has developed by chance is as probable as if a tornado would visit a scrap yard and be able to assemble a fully functional car in the process.

27. APHORISMS

HEREBY SOME shorter reflections on the subject at hand, Integral Esotericism, spirituality and Perennialism.

∼

Do you need "proof of God?" I can't give it to you in writing, but in person—in your own being. So I'd say, go and look yourself in the mirror and if you see some kind of life, some kind of spiritual spark in the eye, then you see "God experiencing himself in us". The Swedish poet Frans Michael Franzén (1772-1847) expressed this "seeing yourself in the mirror" idea in the following way.

It's in the poem *Människans anlete* (*The Face of Man*). I can't render this metrically and poetically in English. But here's the gist: if someone says "there's no soul in the objects, all is dust," to them the poet has the advice: see yourself in the mirror. Even in nature you can see the Spirit embodied in creatures and things, if you only have eyes to see.

We see the same idea in The Upanishads. In section 8.8 of *Chândogya Upanishad* the teacher admonishes his disciples to see themselves in a bowl of water, the mirror of old times. The disciples say that they see their Self, the Âtman. Then the teacher says that this Âtman, this whole brilliance of their essence is equal to God, to Brahman.

I can only repeat: see yourself in the mirror and what do you see, some spark perhaps, some signs of life. That twinkle in the eye. That's the proof of God. That—and the ability of every man to say to himself, "I Am".

⁓

Plotinus called the law of karma "adrasteia," "the inescapable".

⁓

Nietzsche: "Nur wer sich wandelt bleibt mit mir verwandt." This is untranslatable, but the meaning is: "Only he who evolves is akin to me."

⁓

Seek tranquility and stillness. Stillness is eternally true—for it's a mirror of the Primeval Stillness of Logos, of Emptiness, of *Shûnyatâ*. A silent lake under the night sky is a symbol of this, of how still everything really is, in the inner mind. For the movement you otherwise see is there only because of your outer senses being hooked to the world and moving with it. But your inner mind is always still, always quiet, always tranquil, embedded in *samatva* and *apateia*.

⁓

Don't go to heaven, instead realize heaven on earth. This is about "immanentizing the eschaton," as R. A. Wilson, Terence McKenna and others have said.

Hidden consonance is better than open: "heard melodies are sweet, but those unheard are sweeter," as Keats said.

You have to be an Aristocrat of the Soul exerting order, not a Chaos Man exerting chaos. And truly, these are chaotic, decadent times. The Chaotic Mindset rules seemingly supreme. So then, how is it to be an Aristocrat of the Soul in this time of decay? What does it mean today to be an esotericist having order within; how does he project this order to the outside world? Does he even do it; is he maybe satisfied with being a quietist, reclining in splendid isolation? This is also feasible. To abstain from direct action is also a way of acting. The Aristocrat of the Soul is the key figure of today, when the esoteric and mythical forces are rejuvenated. Kâli Yuga is over, Sat Yuga is here, an era dedicated to art, science and spirituality.

Sense perceptions can't be located in space. Why? For instance, in Spinoza's terms, no one has seen the underlying substances. Put differently, perception is an inner phenomenon. "The world is our conception" (Schopenhauer).

Plotinus maintained that the Earth is alive. It's the concept of "Mother Earth," of Gaia, Erda etc. She has an aura like us, a soul like us and she has senses, however, no sensory organs. The Earth is alive. She hears our prayers; she may not have organs but she has senses.

Metaphysics has ultimately to be understood by intuition and higher reason. If you try to explain it with formal logic you end up in mental sterility, like in medieval scholasticism.

∼

As I said in chapter fourteen the concept of the Threefold Flame can give you the basics for a hands-on ethic. How shall I act? By focusing on Will, Truth and Compassion. And with this flame image, acknowledge the essence of will in the *blue* flame, a symbol for the power to run the body; acknowledge the essence of wisdom in the *yellow* flame, nourishing the mind, the flame of illumination; acknowledge the essence of compassion in the *rose* flame, the energy of spiritual love.

∼

Some words on the nature of Christianity. As chapters 12-13 show I want to discuss aspects of Christian mysticism. As for Christianity in general I have an inkling that this religion is somewhat unpopular these days. Now, I'm not planning to preach the overall advantages of this religion. It's a free world, practice what faith you wish. And as for official Christianity I admit that it needs reforming—it needs to become more spiritual and less ritualistic, less mythologically focused on the Gospel Narrative per se. Having said that, I think that many today conceive Christianity wrongly as some sort of hippie religion, some sort of slacker creed where anything goes. This, at least, is a misconception.

Jesus Christ was no hippie preaching hedonism. Instead, he urged people to find the light within ("God is within you", Luke 17:21). His community of disciples and their women was no gang of libertines; it was a serious study group, a band of esotericists living their creed. Christ was no smiling, hugging hippie type; he could be fierce also, saying things like, "I have not come to bring peace, but a sword" (Matthew 10:34). Of course he preached that we should love each other like brethren, this was his defining wisdom, but he wasn't a carefree dandy telling people to go with the flow and do as they pleased, enjoying life in a materialist fashion. Instead, he told people to turn away from materialism and start building the City of God within us, eventually being able to project it around us.

Here it can be noted that Christ didn't expressly tell us to "stop sinning" or "to repent" but to exert "metanoia" (to think differently). See for instance the Greek originals of Matthew 4:17 and Mark 6:12.

∽

"There is no past or future in the universe—there's only energy. And energy has only here and now. An endless and ever-present here and now." Carlos Castaneda, according to the site Cleargreen Workshops

∽

A classical zen question is: look at the flag and tell me what is moving, the flag our your senses? The esoteric, inner answer is of course: the senses. These, the "outer mind," tend to go with the flow of the everyday world. But the inner mind is always essentially tranquil.

In this respect movement and change are unreal, stillness is real.

So if you see a door standing slamming, then *be* the hinge of that door. Be the motionless in the moving, the constancy of the variance, the movement as a state. And if you act, seek rest in action. Meditate by acting, thus shaping your life in the Borderline between a vita activa and a vita contemplativa. Live your creed in every second, every moment. Live your life as a constant operation, constantly characterized by inspiration, initiation and inebriation. Everything is eternally present in the here and now. With willpower you strive for Light, Order and Beauty. The mantra is: "I am truth, I am will, I am passion."

Hume's law tells us: there's no way to derive an *ought* from an *is*, no way to derive values from empirical facts. What, then, is an empirical fact? The trouble of locating sense-perceptions in space is acknowledged by science. Thus, everything is interpretation, everything is ultimately based on preconceived values.

∼

In chapter five I looked at reductionism in natural science and technology. In social sciences and the humanities, for their part, the attitude of reductionism is often expressed in a syndrome called "nothing buttery". This would be exemplified in sayings like, "religion is nothing but morals," "modern art is nothing but graffiti" etc.

∼

> We are formed by our thoughts. Therefore, mind your thought. Words are secondary but thoughts travel far. Every thought we think is colored by our character. (Vivekânanda)

In the same vein, Marcus Aurelius: "The important is not what happens us in life but what we think of it."

∼

When you die some say that everything becomes dark, others say that you meet a Being of Light. For some it darkens, for some it brightens.

∼

Nothing exists and everything.

Jung: "Life is not a problem to solve, it's a mystery to experience."

~

As for man in general, it's said that energy patterns in his mind projects phenomena like architecture, religious systems and politics. The physical, emotional and spiritual life of man is expressed by his mind. This according to the idea of "the Seven Rays," elaborated upon by Alice Bailey and others.

~

Plotinus had a concept called the World Soul. This was somewhat akin to the Holy Ghost of Christian thought, the divine all-soul in its descended form. This World Soul has to partition itself for individual beings, "since these due to their being partitioned cannot receive the soul without its splitting" (Plotinus). If there's no body no soul can emerge in the everyday world; therefore the body exists.

~

You could say: life meets the form and then consciousness emerges. Consciousness is the relation of life to the form.

From the mineral kingdom and up we see successively higher forms of consciousness expressing themselves. It goes from weak and reactive in the mineral, to a certain ability to react to the environment in the plant. Further, the consciousness of animals is demonstrated in *instinct*, and the consciousness of man is *self-consciousness*. He is Homo Sapiens Sapiens, the man who knows that he knows.

According to esoteric theory, a soul is successively, through the aeons, reincarnated through the mineral, plant and animal kingdoms up to the human realm. For its part, the existence in the mineral kingdom is sleepy, the plant existence is somewhat more alive as is, in its turn, the animal existence. Then the soul reaches self-consciousness as a man. To this we have the saying: "The soul sleeps in the stone, dreams in the plant, awakes in the animal and becomes self-conscious in man."

∼

Without law no freedom, without freedom no law.

∼

Everything connects and yet it doesn't.

∼

Antoine de Saint-Exupéry: "A heap of stones ceases to be a heap of stones when the person looking at it within himself carries the image of a cathedral."

CODA

In the introduction I said that this book was an attempt to unify God with Man, mind with matter and reason with intuition—among other things. Well then, have I succeed in this venture? I don't know. These were indeed bold claims and I admitted this even in the Introduction. But an ambition like this has to be embraced in the current, listless and stagnant condition of mankind. And overall I'd say, the way this is going to succeed, to rejuvenate things in a spiritual fashion, for mankind to have a more energetic culture, is by *willpower*. Of willpower I spoke in chapter fourteen. To exert one's will means *to will the good*. Desire, for its part, is inclined toward the dark and the materialistic. I've already said this in this book. Now I stress it again.

If you want a brighter future for earth and man you have to will it. It's that simple. But the simple is difficult, as Clausewitz said. Willpower is the key to liberate earth from the current regime of pessimism, passivity and paranoia. We are co-creators of reality with God. So don't sit down and wait for things to happen, instead, act in the spirit of willpower, envisioning a Reign of Light, acknowledging the Inner Light which is part of the Eternal Light. This is the esoteric way, the holistic modus operandi; it always has been and always will be.

WORDLIST

Hereby a list of words and concepts employed in this study.

~

- *C3* – "Calm, Cool and Collected". Reaching tranquility and mental harmony in a modern way, rooted in tradition. Reaching *samatva, apateia* and *désinvolture*. Q.v. chapter fifteen.
- *C.f.* – Latin *confer*, English commonly *compare*. The latter meaning is applied in this book.
- *Chaotic Mindset* – sported by materialists, nihilists, defeatists. People with a Chaotic Mindset have chaos within and then project it to their environment. The Chaotic Mindset is cured with spiritual outreach activities and enlightenment. Q.v. chapter seventeen.
- *Here-and-Now* – one of the key concepts of the esoteric ethic discussed in this book. It's about living in an eternal now, an infinite here. Q.v. chapter fourteen.
- *Holism* – one of the basic concepts of the esotericist creed. Holism is about seeing wholes, the big picture. Opposite:

reductionism, q.v. chapter five.
- *I Am* – a saying by Christ in The Gospel of John. Ethically, saying "I Am" is about realizing your spiritual Self by way of Rudolf Steiner's interpretation of Christology. See chapters twelve and fourteen.
- *In nuce* – Latin, "in a nut" = in a nutshell.
- *NAMO* – "Napoleonic Modus Operandi," the Napoleonic way of operating. This concept is expressed in the Napoleonic motto: "On s'engage et puis on verra". The meaning is to get going, engage yourself in the action and thus having the situation clarify itself as it develops, affected by your own actions. To be prepared is always important but you sooner or later reach a point where no more preparations can be done, you simply have to get going in order to grasp the big picture. This is in some way related to Cyril Falls' concept of "readiness to fight for information". On NAMO, see chapter sixteen.
- *Perennial* – of Latin *perennis* meaning eternal.
- *Primordial* – primary, fundamental, being or happening first.
- *Q.v.* – Latin *quod vide* = for which see.
- *RAWALTAFA* – this is an acronym for: "Rather Acting Wrongly And Learning Than Abstaining From Action". Ethically, it's better to use "trial and error" than conceiving morals as an abstract problem. See chapter sixteen.
- *Samsâra* – Sanskrit for "confluence," ethically understood as the succession of birth and rebirth of men and all types of living creatures. Ontologically, samsâra is to be seen as the meta-existence of parallel worlds, and of the life of the individual in relation to this Omniverse.
- *School Science, School Physics* – my term for the "official" science of today. It's an example of the "normal science" that Thomas Kuhn (1922-1996) spoke about, the defining way of doing scientific research, defining the current paradigm. Over and above the adopted theories etc. school science is an agreed way of speaking, a way of conducting

yourself verbally and socially. For instance, a current scientist speaking of "metaphysics" or "higher levels of reality" will be shut out of the community for speaking the wrong language, but he may get along if he defines his ideas in terms of "different dimensions" or "multiverse". School physics/science/philosophy is what is taught in the Academy. I've created the concept on the pattern of "school medicine," the art of curing people taught in med school. And along with school medicine we today have "alternative medicine," also known as "complementary medicine" (like acupuncture, homeopathy, using leeches for wound healing, Ayurvedic medicine etc.), practices that today have a semi-acknowledged status (like it's possible for people on Swedish public medcare to be treated by an alternative clinic if he so wishes). With this pattern, the alternative attitudes in physics could be labeled as "complementary physics" so as to ease the transition to the new paradigm. Holism doesn't totally replace school physics, it includes its observations and merely adds new aspects and concepts. That's the nature of a paradigm shift in the Thomas Kuhn sense.

- *Sein* – German for "being," "reality". Sein is the superior reality, and in this creatures, "beings" etc. exist – *Seiendes*, this word being the present participle, plural, of *Sein*. Therefore, using the German concept instead of the English one is more clarifying, for instance, by saying: "we're all *Seiendes im Sein*" than saying "we're all beings in being", which is vague and confusing. The Latin is also of help here: an "essence in esse" is a fine translation for "ein Seiende im Sein".
- *Self, the* – the spirit, soul, essence of man; Sanskrit, Âtman.
- *Urbild* – German for primeval image. Synonym to Platonic idea and form. *Urbild* is the singular form, *Urbilder* the plural.

SOURCES

Religious Documents

A Vedic Reader for Students. Edited by Arthur Anthony MacDonell. Oxford University Press, London 1917
Bhagavad-Gîtâ As It Is. Bhaktivedanta Book Trust, Los Angeles 1983
Den Poetiska Eddan. Translated into Swedish by Björn Collinder. Forum 1972
Plotinus: Mystikern och reformatorn, valda delar av Enneaderna. Translated by Gunnar Rudberg. Bonniers, Stockholm 1927
Shankarâcarya: Upadeshasâhasrî. Madras, India, 1949
The Holy Bible. New King James Version. Thomas Nelson, Inc., Nashville 1982

Monographies, Biographies, Factbooks etc.

Abelar, Taisha: The Sorcerer's Crossing. Viking Books 1992
Agerskov, Michael: Vandra mot ljuset (Danish original, Vandrer mot lyset, 1916). Amelins förlag 1995

Almqvist, Kurt: Att läsa Jung. Natur & Kultur, Stockholm 1997
- Tidlös besinning i en besinningslös tid. Stockholm 1973
Ambjörnsson, Ronny (ed): Bilderboken. Gidlunds 1975
Andersson, Jan S. and Mattsson, Nils-Göran: Filosofisk tanke. Bokförlaget Borken, Borkhult 1988
Balogh, Béla: Den yttersta verkligheten (English original, Ultimate Reality – The New Paradigm of Life Eternal). Svenska White Eagle Lodge, Ljung 1999
Barrow, John D.: The Constants of Nature. From Alpha to Omega. Vintage, Random House, London 2002
- Theories of Everything. The Quest for Ultimate Explanation. Oxford University Press, London 1990
Bergman, Ingmar: Laterna Magica. Norstedts, Stockholm 1987
Bergquist, Lars: Swedenborgs hemlighet. Om Ordets betydelse, änglarnas liv och tjänsten hos Gud. En biografi. Natur & Kultur, Stockholm 1999
Bideau, Paul-Henri: Goethe (Que sais-je). P.U.F. 1984
Bohm, David: Wholeness and the Implicate Order. Routledge 2002
Carlgren, Frans: Den antroposofiska kunskapsvägen. Larson, Täby 1980
Castaneda, Carlos: The Teachings of Don Juan. Arkana 1968
- A Separate Reality. Penguin Arkana 1971
- Journey to Ixtlan. Arkana 1972
- *Castaneda, Carlos:* Tales of Power. Simon & Shuster 1974
Crowley, Vivianne: Principles of Jungian Spirituality. Thorsons, 1998
Davies, Paul: God and the New Physics. Simon & Schuster 1987
- The Mind of God. Simon & Schuster UK 1993
Eliot, T. S.: Collected Poems 1909-1962. Faber & Faber 2002
Evola, Julius: Ride the Tiger (1961). Inner Traditions 2003
Fischer, Hugo: Die Aktualität Plotins: über die Konvergenz von Wissenschaft und Metaphysik. C. H. Beck, München 1956
Gleick, James: Chaos: Making a New Science. 1987
Green, Brian: The Fabric of the Cosmos: Space, Time and the Texture of Reality. Alfred A. Knopf, New York 2007
Gustafsson, Lars: Landskapets långsamma förändringar. Natur &

Kultur, Stockholm 1992
Jung, Carl: Mitt liv (*Erinnerungen, Träume, Gedanke,* 1961; English edition as *Memories, Dreams, Reflections*). Natur & Kultur, Stockholm 1964
Jünger, Ernst: Jahre der Okkupation. Ernst Klett Verlag, Stuttgart 1958
- Typus, Name, Gestalt. Ernst Klett Verlag, Stutttgart 1963
Jünger, Ernst: Über die Linie. Klostermann, Frankfurt 1950
Kaim, Lore (ed): Goethe – Gedichte. Volk und Wissen Verlag, Berlin 1949
Kranz, Gisbert: Ernst Jüngers symbolische Weltschau. Pädagogische Verlag Schwann, Hamburg 1968
Lagercrantz, Olof: Dikten om livet på andra sidan. Månpocket, Stockholm 1997
Laurency, Henry T.: De vises sten: världs- och livskunskap. Laurency, Skövde 1995
Neaman, Elliot: A Dubious Past – Ernst Jünger and the Politics of Literature After Nazism. University of California Press, Los Angeles 1999
Nevin, Thomas: Ernst Jünger and Germany: Into the Abyss, 1914-1945. Constable & Co, London 1997
Nilsson, Albert: Svensk romantik – den platonska strömningen. Gleerups, Lund 1964
Noll, Richard: The Jung Cult. 1997
Random, Michel: Japan – Strategy of the Unseen. Crucible, Wellingborough (GB), 1987
Safranski, Rüdiger: Nietzsche – A Philosophical Biography. W W Norton & Company 2003
Schuré, Edouard: Hermes och Mose. Skoglund, Stockholm 1910. (A translated excerpt from Schuré's Magnum Opus *Les grands initiés. Esquisse de l'histoire secrète des religions,* 1889, which had chapters on Hermes and Moses as well as Râma, Krishna, Orpheus, Pythagoras, Plato and Jesus. The English edition is called *The Great Initiates. A Study of the Secret History of Religions.*)
Schuré, Edouard: Tre stora siare: Orfeus, Platon, Jesus. Almqwist & Wiksell, Uppsala 1924. (A similar excerpt as the above.)

Sheldrake, Rupert: Utvecklingslära *in* Peter Brookesmith (ed), Att tänka det otänkbara (*Thinking the Unexplained,* 1983). Bokorama, Höganäs 1988
Shepherd, A. P.: Rudolf Steiner och antroposofin (*A Scientist of the Invisible,* 1957). Natur & Kultur, Stockholm 1974
Smith, E. E.: The Epic of Space in Lloyd Arthur Eschenbach (ed), Of Worlds Beyond: The
Science of Science Fiction Writing. Fantasy Press 1947
Spengler, Oswald: Västerlandets undergång – konturer till en morfologi om världshistorien. 1. Gestalt och verklighet 2. Världshistoriska perspektiv (*Der Untergang des Abendlandes – Umrisse einer Morphologie der Weltgeschichte,* 1918-1922). Atlantis, Stockholm 1996
Steiner, Rudolf: Grunddragen i vetenskapen om det fördolda (*Die Geheimwissenschaft im Umriss,* 1925). Antroposofiska bokförlaget 1979
 - Johannesevangeliet (*Das Johannes-Evangelium,* 1908). Antroposofiska bokförlaget, 1959
Svensson, Lennart: Ernst Jünger – A Portrait. Manticore Press, Melbourne, 2014
Swedenborg, Emanuel: Drömboken. Walhström & Widstrand 1952
Sällström, Pehr: Goethe och naturvetenskapen. Carlsson bokförlag, 1993
Södergran, Edith: Samlade dikter. Wahlström & Widstrand 1996
Wilber, Ken (ed): The Holographic Paradigm and Other Paradoxes. Shambhala 1982
Wald, George: Self-Intellection and Identity in the Philosophy of Plotinus. University of California, 1987
Weil, Simone: La pesanteur et la grâce. 1947

News Articles

Bornstein, Anna *in* Svenska Dagbladet 18/4 1988: Granskog – en kosmisk tanke?
Eriksson, Karl-Erik *in* Dagens Nyheter 1/2 1987: Hem till kaos

- 3/2 1987: Trygghetens demon går upp i rök
- Dagens Nyheter 4/2 1987: Fräls oss från Tomgångsmessias

Jakubowski, Jackie *in* Dagens Nyheter 26/3 2004: Om pi varit 3,141591...

Sidenbladh, Erik *in* Svenska Dagbladet 88-07-10: På spaning efter en ny världsbild
- 11/7 1988: Hjärnan är ett cocktailparty
- 12/7 1988: Från rädsla till en lek med många möjligheter
- 13/7 1988: Nu återupptäcker vi tiden

INDEX OF PERSONS

BOHM, David, 76

DAVIES, Paul, 68, 72, 76

DESCARTES, René, 23, 32, 35, 36, 49, 56, 200

DRIESCH, Hans, 38, 50

ELIOT, T. S., 13, 16, 114, 138, 180-186

ERIKSSON, Karl-Erik, 53-55, 77-78

FISCHER, Hugo, 38, 50-52, 75-76, 81-84

FRIEDRICH, C. D., 13, 16, 20, 21, 156, 159, 187-193

GOETHE, J. W., 13, 15, 16, 20, 26, 28-30, 32, 38, 41-46, 83, 125, 127, 196, 199, 204, 205, 210

GREEN, Brian, 63-67

HUXLEY, T. H., 61, 79, 80

JUNG, Carl, 13, 16, 20, 26, 71, 74, 87, 107, 120, 127, 145-155, 180, 210, 220

JÜNGER, Ernst, 16, 26, 27, 29, 30, 32, 38, 44, 50, 119, 127, 128, 134, 140, 150, 155, 164, 165, 177, 199, 203-206, 210

KANT, Immanuel, 23, 79

NIETZSCHE, Friedrich, 13, 16, 20, 38, 107, 117, 124, 141, 151, 156-173, 177, 178, 180, 184, 190, 215

PLOTINUS, 11, 13, 14-16, 18-29, 31-33, 41, 42, 50, 51, 71-73, 75, 76, 85, 127, 148, 199, 200, 215, 216, 220

SHELDRAKE, Rupert, 29, 59-60

STEINER. Rudolf, 13, 85, 86, 93-113, 122, 123, 144, 208

SWEDENBORG, Emanuel, 13, 16, 155, 199-202

SÖDERGRAN, Edith, 16, 20, 31, 73, 138, 173-180

ABOUT THE AUTHOR

LENNART SVENSSON (1965-) made his English language debut in 2014 with *Ernst Jünger – A Portrait*. This was followed in 2015 by a bio on another illustrious German, Richard Wagner. In Swedish Svensson has published a number of essays along with some novels. He's currently working on several novels and essays in English. He lives in northern Sweden and has a BA in Indology.

www.ingramcontent.com/pod-product-compliance
Lightning Source LLC
Chambersburg PA
CBHW032250150426
43195CB00008BA/391